planting
hope
here

Rosario Picardo and Shannon Kiser

planting
hope
here

Cultivating Faith Community with Those
on the Recovery Journey

Plano, Texas

Planting Hope Here: Cultivating Faith Community with Those on
the Recovery Journey

Copyright 2026 by Rosario Picardo and Shannon Kiser

This book is printed on acid-free, elemental chlorine-free paper.

ISBN: Paperback 978-1-963265-90-3; eBook 978-1-963265-91-0

26 27 28 29 30 31 32 33 34 35—10 9 8 7 6 5 4 3 2 1
MANUFACTURED IN THE UNITED STATES OF AMERICA

About the Authors

S tarting a new Christian community within the recovery space is a noble calling as well as a powerful way to accompany people with hope and healing as they journey a difficult road. This resource is an attempt to offer a bit of a "road map" to help you prayerfully develop, build, and establish a thriving Jesus-shaped recovery community.

I (Shannon) first encountered the ripple effects of addiction in high school. A dear classmate struggling with an absent father found that drugs numbed the pain of his abandonment. He went from recreational user to full blown addict quickly and never found his way out of that stronghold. I always wondered if his story could have turned out differently in the context of a hopeful and healing community. When Jesus announced his ministry to the religious community, he declared that his ministry would include release for the captives. Embedded in that proclamation was a challenge for the religious elite…are you burdening people or freeing people? Many of our traditional churches, as earnestly welcoming as they want to be, do not feel like safe and hopeful environments for those in recovery or families rocked by addiction. Yet, what if we were to join up with Jesus' heart for people and foster faith community that meets people right where they are and walks with them towards Jesus' invitation of hope and healing. I do not profess to be an expert on recovery, but I share my experiences helping churches and everyday Christians discover how God might be calling them into the everyday spaces of life to be signposts of the gospel in a world needing to encounter grace.

I (Roz) never thought about recovery ministry of any sort until I entered the world of church planting. While planting my first church fresh out of seminary, I roomed with a guy who was in recovery. It was an adjustment for both of us because he was now roommates with a crazy church planter. "John" was my first recruit on the launch team. One evening, as I was returning home from an evening out with a friend, I noticed my car was missing from the driveway, along with my roommate. Unfortunately, "John" had relapsed and sold my car to a drug dealer for $20. I still had the title to the vehicle, tracked it down, and reclaimed it. Yet, the car incident showed me the reality of addiction and revealed to me that my ministry call would be focused on recovery. I share my experiences primarily as a practitioner who has made numerous mistakes and has also witnessed God move in remarkable ways. I offer these experiences not as a "one-size-fits-all" approach, but rather as examples to learn from as you conduct the contextual analysis.

Introduction

It is no secret that we are in the fight for people's lives amidst the drug epidemic. Drug use and other forms of addiction have touched almost every facet of our society. As I (Roz) moved to Dayton, OH, and launched Mosaic Church, in 2017 my city was in the headlines as the highest per capita opioid overdose mortality rate in the United States. We prayed that God would use our new church to respond to such a crisis. And four years later, Fighting Chance Recovery was born, a faith-based recovery worship gathering and community, which has seen countless lives transformed, families healed, and people walking with Jesus. My heart is to see other church, teams, and Jesus-followers make a difference when it comes to starting their own fresh expression of recovery.

As co-authors of this book, Shannon and I share the same heart. While each of us brings a different experience to the conversation, we both recognize that new forms of Christian community are needed to engage with the culture in which we now find ourselves. Courageous followers of Jesus are being sent out to incarnate his grace and healing in the nooks and crannies of everyday life—and it is our hope that you are some of those courageous disciples.

This resource is focused specifically on ministry with the recovery community and the loved ones and neighborhoods affected by addiction. It is meant to be a traveling companion as you discern what God might be inviting you to do. It is not a formula, but rather a set of principles, examples, and considerations for you to explore as you seek to start a fresh expression of church with those navigating the recovery journey. Think of it less like a blueprint and more like a Polaroid picture slowly coming into focus. As you spend time among the recovery community exploring some of the questions in this resource, what begins as a blur of possibilities gradually reveals the contours of God's invitation.

The Missional Journey of Fresh Expressions

What do you picture when you think of "church?" Is it a sanctuary with pews? Or a familiar liturgical flow? What if it could look like a community of prayer after an Alcoholics Anonymous meeting, or a circle of friends who show up for each other in the heartache of relapse? These are holy spaces too.

That's what Fresh Expressions are all about. They are new forms of Christian community that take shape in the middle of real life, whether that's a neighborhood, a coffee shop, or a network of people who share a common struggle and a common hope. Instead of asking people to come to our church, Fresh Expressions make space for people to encounter Jesus in their world, in rhythms that connect with their hurts and hopes.

For those walking the journey of addiction and recovery, this matters deeply. A coffee bar conversation might feel superficial, a polished liturgy might feel inaccessible, and upbeat worship songs might not match the heaviness of the road ahead. But in the gritty honesty of recovery, Jesus meets people with freedom, hope, and a faith community that truly understands. The Body of Christ can take root right there, in the fragile but beautiful places where people are reaching for new life.

The process through which this kind of contextually shaped community emerges is described in the Fresh Expressions movement as the Missional Journey:

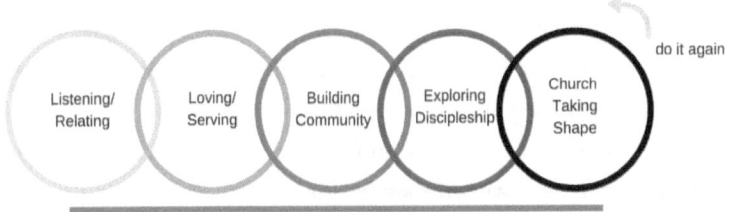

undergirded by prayer and ongoing listening

Every Fresh Expression begins with *listening*. We listen to God in prayer and to the community around us with presence. Listening helps us notice the hopes and hurts of this place, and it also helps us see where God is already at work. You're not bringing Jesus to people; he's already here. Listening just tunes your ears to how he might be inviting you to join in.

As you linger and show up, *love* begins to flow naturally. Friendships form slowly, maybe even awkwardly at first, but they grow real over time. You'll find yourself sharing meals, hearing stories, and learning the language of this community. In recovery spaces, this often looks like mutual care, being honest about struggle, celebrating small victories, and staying present through setbacks.

Over time, individual friendships start to knit together. What was once a handful of connections begins to look like a web of relationships. Community takes root. People discover a sense of "home" with one another, maybe for the first time in a long time.

Because you've shown up as your authentic self, people already know you're a follower of Jesus. That opens natural opportunities to explore faith together—without pressure and without pretense. It could be a conversation after a meeting, a shared prayer before dinner, or a story from Scripture that resonates with someone's lived experience. These small steps become entry points for practicing life in God's kingdom together.

As faith deepens, something beautiful happens. The community begins to anchor itself in Christ, and a new kind of church starts to emerge. It may not look exactly like the Sunday morning gathering with which you are most familiar, but it is one shaped by the rhythms of recovery life. Prayer, worship, generosity, and mutual care spring up right there in everyday spaces. The Body of Christ.

Keeping this journey in mind will help you stay grounded. It's not about starting a worship service for the recovery community but about cultivating a Jesus-shaped community with the recovery community. Throughout this guide, you'll hear echoes of this journey again and again. It will serve as both a compass and a check-in: Are mutual friendships forming? Is community deepening? Is your listening shaping the way you love? Are you noticing places of spiritual curiosity? When things stall or feel stuck, come back to the missional journey. This framework will remind you where you might need to refocus or lean in again.

What to Expect

Starting this journey can feel a little like holding a Polaroid photo fresh out of the camera. At first, the picture is blurry—just a hazy outline of what might be. You don't quite know what you're looking at yet, but something is there.

That's how this process begins. As you practice prayerful listening, the faint outlines start to emerge. Then come the early decision points: Who will you show up with? Where will you spend your time? How will you lean into the relationships forming around you? Each choice sharpens the picture a little more.

Over time, what was once vague comes into focus. You begin to see signs of community, friendship, faith, and even church life taking shape. It won't be instant, and it won't look like a glossy print from a professional photographer. But slowly, with patience and faithfulness, the image becomes clear: a community anchored in Jesus living out healing together.

Our hope is that this planting guide will help you hold that Polaroid steady as the picture comes into view. And we trust that, through your presence, listening, and courage, the image that emerges will look a lot like the faith community God longs to form.

You are stepping into holy, gritty, beautiful work. We are praying for you as you take each step. Now, let's get started.

Begin With A Listening Posture

The LORD came and stood there, calling as at the other times, "Samuel! Samuel!" Then Samuel said, "Speak, for your servant is listening."
—*1 Samuel 3:10*

S o, you want to start a new form of Christian community among the recovery community? It's tempting to start with a broad target group, a marketing plan, and an order of worship. Churches are notorious for coming up with their great new ideas and launching into initiatives without ever stopping to explore whether anyone outside their congregation thinks it is a great idea. Or whether it aligns with the heart of God.

When Ron Johnson, the former Apple executive, became CEO of JCPenney, he attempted a dramatic overhaul. Believing he knew what customers wanted without getting to know any, he eliminated coupons, slashed sales, and rebranded the store with a clean, modern aesthetic. Johnson assumed that JCPenney's core shoppers wanted an Apple-like retail experience with an elevated and streamlined ethos. But he never really listened to the people who shopped at JCPenney—longtime customers who loved the thrill of sales, the reliability of discounts, and the feeling of getting a deal. Within two years, sales plummeted by 25 percent, billions were lost, and Johnson was ousted. The business had been redesigned based on a compelling idea, but without resonance or relationship with the audience. Too often, churches approach launching new ministries—especially something as sacred and sensitive as recovery ministry—like JCPenney's failed reinvention: with good intentions, a clever brand, and strategic ambition, but no actual listening. They start with a plan before they start with people.

Especially in the realm of recovery, that approach can do real harm. People in recovery have stories marked by vulnerability, pain, shame and regret. A church that wants to walk alongside them must do more than offer a program or a worship service. It must earn trust. And that starts not with assumptions, but with attentive listening.

Before launching that new ministry, what if you paused long enough to walk the neighborhood, sit in on open meetings, grab coffee with local counselors, talk to people in recovery? Not as "target participants," but as wise companions. What if you asked more questions than you answered?

You might discover that the need isn't a worship service at all, but a safe space for storytelling. Or a midweek meal. Or someone to show up at court. You might learn that "recovery" isn't a marketing niche. It's holy ground. Mission is not about what we think people need. It's about discovering, through listening, what God might already be doing and joining in. If we want to foster meaningful mission among the recovery community, it is critical to lead with humility and not just a bunch of hype.

Letting Prayer Shape Our Posture

The movement from "launching a ministry" to becoming a people who are safe and present for those in recovery is deeply spiritual work. It cannot be rushed. And it cannot be faked. Prayer is our formation ground—not just a way to bless the ministry after it's planned, but the very way we become the kind of people God can entrust with a mission like this.

Below are several concrete prayer practices that can shape leaders and teams with a posture of humility, compassion, and readiness. As you prepare to start a ministry with the recovery or recovery adjacent community, the very best place you can start is listening prayer.

Increasing Awareness and Compassion

Gather a friend or two and take a walk around a section of your community that God might be inviting you to walk and pray. As you walk, begin to notice things that may have been hidden in plain sight when you were not paying attention. Are there signs of addiction's ripple effects: drug paraphernalia, empty bottles, boarded up homes, payday loan offices, security cameras, Narcan boxes, graffiti, suicide hotline flyers? What else?

Ask:

God, what pain and longings might these places carry?
Whose story is told—or untold—here?

Linger near places of pain or hope. If you pass a hospital, clinic, jail, school, bar, or church—pause. Let it become a prayer station:

Jesus, you walked among the brokenhearted.
Walk among the brokenhearted in this place.
Bring freedom to the captive.
Bring comfort to the child who is afraid.
Bring hope to the parent who is exhausted.
Bring peace to the one who is using tonight just to survive.

Maybe you begin to notice that addiction doesn't just affect the individual, it impacts children, grandparents, teachers, employers, first responders, and more.

Pause and ask:

> *God, show me the unseen grief. Show me the strength of those who carry more than they can bear.*

Pray for families:

> *Bind up the brokenhearted. Restore what has been lost.*

As your walk ends, sit or stand in silence for a moment.

Ask:

What surprised me?

What stirred my compassion?

Where did I sense your presence?

Prayers of Proximity

Commit to praying regularly in the places where recovery happens—outside treatment centers, near halfway houses, or in coffee shops where support groups meet. Let the location inform the prayer.

God, open our eyes to what you're doing here. Teach us to see with your eyes.

Intercessory Listening

Rather than praying for those in recovery from a distance, enter spaces where they are telling their stories, such as open recovery meetings. Afterward, sit silently before God and allow God to deepen your awareness.

Reflect:

What did I feel?

Where did I sense God's presence?

What surprised or unsettled me?

Scripture-Focused Prayer on Jesus' Posture

Explore gospel passages where Jesus encounters people on the margins—especially those society labeled unclean or unworthy—Pray slowly through them using, noticing the words or phrases that stick out for you.

Some good starting texts:

Luke 7:36–50 (the woman who anoints Jesus)

John 5:1–15 (healing by the pool)

Luke 19:1-10 (Zacchaeus the tax collector)

Ask:

What does Jesus see?

How does he respond?

What would it mean to mirror this posture?

Prayers of Repentance and Receptivity

Honestly name the fears, prejudices, or discomforts that may rise in you as you consider ministering among those in recovery. Create space for God to gently reshape your heart.

Lord, forgive my assumptions. Heal my desire to fix or control. Teach me to receive people as you do.

Prayer Shapes Mission

One community I (Shannon) worked with wanted to serve people experiencing homelessness and addiction. Rather than immediately launching a program, they committed to forty days of intentional prayer. They met weekly in a local park where many in recovery gathered, simply to walk, listen, and pray silently. No glossy brochures. Just presence and prayer.

Each week, God seemed to draw people into conversation. Over those forty days, this group learned names and built trust. By the end of this intentional season, several in the prayer group were regularly sharing meals with people from the park. Eventually, a new worshiping community was born—not because they launched a program, but because prayer had changed their posture.

Jesus never ministered from a distance. He entered the pain. He noticed the unseen. He wept with the grieving. He restored those struggling with shame. Prayer helps us live and love people from that same heart.

What has God revealed to you through these prayer practices?

Speak, Lord, for we are listening.
Teach us to walk slowly, to listen deeply, and to notice what has
long been hidden in plain sight. Give us hearts shaped by your
presence. Give us postures marked by humility.
Give us eyes to see where you are already at work. Help us to
become people of prayerful presence. May we not rush in to fix but
instead stay long enough to love. In Jesus' name,
Amen.

Listening Deeply in the Community

Therefore if you have any encouragement from being united with Christ, if any comfort from his love, if any common sharing in the Spirit, if any tenderness and compassion, then make my joy complete by being like-minded, having the same love, being one in spirit and of one mind. Do nothing out of selfish ambition or vain conceit. Rather, in humility value others above yourselves, not looking to your own interests but each of you to the interests of others.

—*Philippians 2:1-4*

A few years ago, a group of leaders had a vision: they wanted to do something to serve low-income families in their city. Initially, they thought about offering traditional resources like food, clothes, or childcare—a well-meaning but standard approach. But instead of rushing to launch, they spent time hosting community listening sessions. And what they heard surprised them. Repeatedly, they heard laundry. It wasn't glamorous and it wasn't on anyone's strategic radar. But it was foremost on the mind of the community. And so, The Laundry Project was born.

Imagine if they hadn't listened. They might have launched a tutoring program or a food pantry—good things to be sure, but not the right thing for that moment and community. In the same way, churches often feel drawn to launch recovery ministries because the need is urgent and real. But unless they begin with listening, they may offer what they think is needed instead of what is actually needed.

Community conversations aren't just good strategy. They open us up to stories and perspectives we would not otherwise hear. In addition, they open the door for mission to become mutual, where we are changed just as much as those we hope to engage.

Who Might Be Good Conversation Partners?

Start by making a list of who might make good conversation partners. Perhaps you want to consider:

People in Recovery – they have lived experience that is important to hear. Consider connecting with those who have been in recovery for some time, as well as those who are early in their recovery journey.

Family Members – especially parents, spouses, or adult children. They also have a lived experience, but from a different angle than those in recovery themselves.

Addiction Counselors / Therapists – Case workers, social workers, reentry program leaders

Emergency medical responders/law enforcement/court officials

Community members in affected neighborhoods

Faith leaders already involved in recovery work

School counselors or youth workers

Develop Thoughtful Questions

Next, prepare some questions or prompts that will help you to listen and learn. For example:

What do you see as the biggest challenges related to addiction in this community?

What are the most common barriers to recovery here?

Are there local organizations or people already doing helpful work in this area?

Where do you see gaps in support—practical, emotional, relational, spiritual?

Where do you see opportunities for a greater sense of joy and belonging?

Who else do you think I should talk with?

For those with a lived experience of addiction or recovery, consider asking questions like these:

What has helped you most in your recovery journey?

What has been unhelpful, even if well-intentioned?

Have you ever tried to find spiritual support during recovery? What was that like?

What do you wish faith communities better understood about addiction?

What would it take for you to trust a church or spiritual group?

What kind of community would feel safe and healing to you?

If you could design a space or gathering that truly supported healing, what would it include?

What words or ideas come to mind when you hear about a "recovery church community"? What excites or concerns you?

What does hope look like to you right now?

Remember that these questions are a starting point, not a check-list. This is not a research project but rather a listening posture. When we can enter these conversations with curiosity and presence, the sharing will naturally flow, and we may be surprised at the profound perspectives we will hear.

In one community I (Shannon) was exploring with a team, it was through similar conversations that we heard that there was not a lack of church programs in the area, it's just that there was not one single church that families navigating addiction felt they could enter and be honest about the messiness of their lives. That understanding helped to shape a new community that could be raw and real before God.

After each conversation, reflect on these questions:

What surprised me in what I heard?

Where did my assumptions get challenged?

What are my big takeaways?

What is God saying to me?

A recovery church community can't start with a logo and a brochure. It must start with listening to God and to the community. When we know names and stories, hopes and heartaches, then we are beginning to set a foundation upon which the Lord can build meaningful community that expresses God's heart.

Gracious God,
You are the God of every story. And you know more deeply the hurts and hopes of our community than we ever could. So, teach us to lead with listening. Open our ears to voices we've overlooked, and our hearts to pain we don't yet understand. May every conversation plant a seed of compassion. May every story deepen our love. And as we listen, may we hear your voice whispering, "This is holy ground." In Jesus' name, Amen.

Assess the Needs and Opportunities

And God is able to bless you abundantly, so that in all things at all times, having all that you need, you will abound in every good work.
—*2 Corinthians 9:8*

Several years back, frozen yogurt shops were all the rage. The first shop or two had lines out the door, filled with people waiting to choose all their tasty toppings. Within a year, there were yogurt shops everywhere you turned. They may have had different décor, but they were all the same basic premise: frozen yogurt, choose your own toppings, pay by weight. Within another year, almost all of them had closed. Why? Because one town did not need that many yogurt shops.

Before starting anything new, it's wise to discover what God is already doing through people, networks, and organizations in the recovery space. There is no need to replicate—nor compete with—the things that already exist. For example, in one community, we heard over and over that there was a perceived need for transitional housing for those coming out of rehabilitation programs. As we dug deeper, we discovered that there were reputable groups already working in this space, with a plan to open up several new houses. Yet, at the same time, there were very few substance-free social spaces for those in recovery to spend free time. That awareness began to shape the direction of the mission that could be most meaningful in that context.

As we explore what already exists, we may find out that almost every church in town is running a Celebrate Recovery worship service. What the town doesn't need, then, is another Celebrate Recovery worship service! The real question is, what might be needed? And the second is this: is it ours to do?

Why All This Research and Discernment, Anyway?

We just want to start a recovery service! Can't we just get on with it?

Here's why it's important to take the time to dig into the needs of the community. We are never just starting a worship service...we are fostering a beloved community. When we start with a band and a sermon series instead of the hopes and dreams and longings of a people, we are likely to start from a place of disconnect.

In addition, this discernment posture may lead us to narrow our focus. Perhaps there are plenty of generic recovery services, but nothing that can really captivate young people struggling to break free of addiction. If that needs to be your focus, the worship design might look wildly different than the service you were initially imagining. Or perhaps by deeply listening, you discover that there is visceral suspicion of church people among the recovery community. It is highly unlikely, then, that offering a recovery service is the best starting point. Instead, the best first step for connection may be a community meal or a group workout.

With this in mind, exploring the needs and opportunities in the community isn't wasted time...it is strategic time.

Clarifying The Opportunities and What Might Be Yours to Do

Asset mapping is the process of identifying and organizing the strengths, resources, gifts, and relationships that already exist within a community or congregation. Rather than starting with problems or deficits, asset mapping begins by asking: "What do we already have? Who is already here? Where is life already flowing?"

Getting clear about that allows us to begin to identify the gaps and opportunities that may exist, followed by an honest assessment of what opportunities might best line up with our gifts, capacity, and relational networks. In other words, missional discernment is less likely to be a lightning bolt from the sky than an adventure of following the nudging of the Holy Spirit towards a hazy destination as we prayerfully explore what we are discovering and what God is stirring in our hearts. So, let's begin to follow those nudges through a framework of guided prompts in four parts.

This process works best if there are several people listening and discerning together. In our next chapter we will look at building a team, but even in this stage, it is helpful to have multiple voices and perspectives at the table.

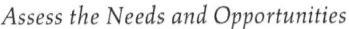

Step One: Consider What Already Exists

Before we create something new, let's honor what's already here.

Who in our community is already walking with people in recovery? (List individuals, organizations, churches, groups, informal networks.)

What kinds of recovery gatherings are already happening? (AA, NA, Celebrate Recovery, SMART Recovery, therapy groups, peer circles, etc.)

Where do people in recovery find safe space, connection, or practical support? (Name the locations—churches, shelters, homes, libraries, parks.)

Are there people in our congregation or community who have lived experience with addiction and recovery? What roles do they play?

What are some places of trust in our city that may not be Christian but are doing healing work?

You may have some ready answers after your community conversations, but these questions might prompt you to do a little bit more research.

Step Two: What Gaps or Struggles Exist?

Now, let's get honest about what's missing, strained, or not working.

> Where do people fall through the cracks? (E.g., after rehab, during housing transitions, when they relapse, etc.)
>
> Who feels forgotten, shamed, or left out by existing efforts?
>
> What resources are hard to access (because of stigma, location, cost, complexity)?
>
> Are there unmet spiritual needs for people in recovery or their families?
>
> What voices are missing in the conversation? (Young people, people of color, families, etc.)

Step Three: Where Are the Opportunities?

> Where do we sense a gentle stirring of the Spirit?
>
> Where do relationships already exist that could be deepened into partnership?
>
> Are there trusted people with lived experience who could help us dream together?
>
> What's one small, relational step we could take (before starting a worship service or building a program)?

Are there overlooked or underused spaces we could offer for connection or rest?

If we could experiment with one act of kindness that built trust—what might it be?

What kind of worship might resonate with the people we've been coming to know?

Pause here and pray:

God, show us where you are already at work—and where you are inviting us to join you.

Step Four: What Is Ours to Do?

Not everything that needs doing is ours to do. Let's honestly explore how we might best be able to come alongside the recovery community in the ways that the Spirit has uniquely wired us.

What strengths or gifts has God already placed in our community? (People with lived experience, hospitality, a kitchen, transportation, deep compassion…)

What do we not have right now? (Training, time, trust, trauma-informed skills…)

When we look at the existing gaps, is there something that calls out to us, breaks our heart, or aligns with a sweet spot for us?

What's one area where we need to learn before we lead?

Are we being invited to start something—or to support and deepen something that already exists?

Making Sense of What You've Discovered

Now that you've walked through the four quadrants—naming what exists, identifying the gaps, exploring opportunities, and prayerfully reflecting on what may be yours to do—you likely have a board (or page) full of insight. So, what now?

This is the moment to step back and take a prayerful look at what you've uncovered. Gather your team and talk through these reflection prompts:

> What surprised you as you mapped the landscape?
>
> What patterns or themes do you notice? Is there a group of people who keep getting mentioned?
>
> A shared concern? A repeated challenge?
>
> Where is there energy or momentum already building?
>
> What seems small but sacred—a relational seed you could water?
>
> Where do you sense the Spirit's invitation, not just your own good ideas?

Sometimes the temptation is to leap into trying to solve every problem. But this exercise isn't about solving problems—it's about being attuned to the community, discovering where there might be places of resonance, noticing natural connecting points, and discerning how God might be inviting us to enter into the longings and celebrations of a people, fostering beloved community right there.

Ask:

Out of everything you've surfaced, what won't leave you alone?

Is there a particular injustice, a specific subgroup of people or a specific need that seems to grab your heart?

Pay attention to that and jot it down here. What breaks your heart may be where your mission begins. In addition, write down anything that has been clarified for you as you walked through this exercise.

God of compassion and wisdom,
You are already moving in our community—healing what is broken, lifting up the weary, planting seeds of hope in places we cannot yet see. Thank you for giving us eyes to catch glimpses of what you are doing. Open our eyes and our hearts to become more aware of how you might be inviting us to join in your work of renewal and restoration. Help us not to rush ahead with our own ideas, but to move at the pace of love. Show us what is ours to do, and what is not. Align our gifts with the needs of the community and help us to follow the gentle nudgings of your Spirit. We ask you to guide us one faithful step at a time. In the name of Jesus, our Healer and Friend, Amen.

Chapter 4

Building the Team

There are different kinds of gifts, but the same Spirit distributes them.
There are different kinds of service, but the same Lord. There are differ-
ent kinds of working, but in all of them and in everyone it is the same
God at work. Now to each one the manifestation of the Spirit is given
for the common good.

—1 Corinthians 12:4-7

Now it's time to start thinking about team, if you haven't already. A meaningful recovery ministry is not something that one person can do alone. One recovery initiative started with four people and an old run-down rental warehouse space. One was a former bartender who had seen people in their worst moments. One was an elementary school teacher with a passion for those in the margins. One was an artist able to envision the potential beauty of not just the space but the community that could emerge here. One was a pastor who didn't know much about recovery but knew how to listen and had a natural way with people.

Together, they had walked the community and had heard the stories. Together they prayed, week after week, asking God to show them what to do. They prayed as they worked to make the warehouse space functional. They prayed as they met addicts in the parking lot. They prayed as murals were painted. And they celebrated as God opened the door to purchase Ninja gym equipment at a rock-bottom price, which gave them a clear way forward to create a natural hangout space for those in recovery that they had come to know in their community.

That was the beginning. Nothing more than a team willing to follow God step by step, prayerfully experimenting the way forward. Once the fitness equipment purchase was made, they began to ask: What would it look like to create a safe place for physical exertion? Then, what would it look like to create a safe place for sharing the struggles of life and recovery? Then, what would it look like to create a safe place for faith exploration?

That's the impact of four people with a heart for Jesus and a compassion for those struggling with addiction in their community.

Develop the Heart and Mind of a Team

Living out a ministry in and among the recovery community is going to take more than one committed person—it's going to take a team. So, it's important to gather a group of people who have some energy around the mission to discern and organize for action. However, before roles and schedules, it's important to develop the posture and practices that can develop a healthy DNA within the group. A vibrant team is not just a task force. It's a spiritual community of discerners—people who listen to God, to each other, and to the needs around them. You may find it helpful to embed these practices in your team from the earliest stages:

> Pray regularly together—not just before or at the end of meetings, but as a posture of listening.

> Name what you're noticing in the community and in your own hearts—perhaps you want to start each meeting reflecting on stories of how God is working or where you see hope and healing surfacing.

Practice curiosity instead of control—what might God be inviting us to try?

Debrief and reflect after each experiment—not just what worked, but what stirred your souls.

Celebrate small wins—it's not always about filling a room. "I met someone new today" or "We had a great conversation at my table tonight" is worth celebrating.

You may want to keep a shared journal or document where team members record "God sightings," moments of learning, or stories of impact. Return to it again and again to keep yourselves encouraged and centered in the mission.

Identify Key Roles on the Team

What are the variety of gifts and skill sets that would help this mission to thrive? I (Shannon) once attended a potluck luncheon in which every single contribution was a Jello salad. The luncheon table would have greatly benefitted from a variety of flavors and textures. In the same way, you don't want a team of people who all have the same skill sets. Not everyone needs to do everything—but everyone needs to bring something. In forming a solid team, consider some key roles that could be significant for meaningfully connecting with the recovery community.

1. **The Passionate Connectors**

   The Connectors bring relational energy, ease of connection, and, often, lived experience. Those who can help fulfill this role may already be in relationship with people in recovery or feel a deep calling to this work. They help keep the vision anchored in compassion and authenticity.

2. **The Shepherds**

   Shepherds have a caring presence. They are intentional

about offering spiritual and emotional care for the team and participants because it naturally flows out of them. They can listen without fixing and guide without controlling. They help to foster a caring community that is tender to the spiritual needs of participants.

3. **The Organizers**

   Organizers are skilled in administration and logistics. Every team needs elements of organization, and these are the people who will keep things running smoothly, with an eye on scheduling, communications, and details. They create an environment that frees up others to focus on relationships and spiritual support.

Build a Diverse and Well-Rounded Team

Recovery journeys are layered, so your team should be too. You'll want to think about whether your team reflects the community you are seeking to love and serve if you are to foster a safe and approachable environment for participants to flourish.

You may be tempted to form a team of only people in your congregation. But ask yourself whether there might need to be others engaged in these early stages. Are there others who share your vision and your heart—even if they aren't members in your existing church? Who could be a "bridge of trust" among the people that this mission is meant to engage? Who can help potential participants see a reflection of themselves in the mix? Whose perspectives are needed for you to better understand the recovery journey and form meaningful community?

Pay attention to diversity in:

Lived Experience: Some in recovery, some not—but all humble learners.

Gifts: For example, communication, empathy, hospitality, creativity, wisdom, encouragement.

Demographics: Age, race, economic background, etc.

Personality: Every team needs dreamers and doers, hosts
and hustlers, prophets and peacemakers.

Diversity doesn't happen by accident. Be intentional about who
you invite to the table—and whose voices get amplified.

Foster Energy, Alignment, and Trust

You want a team that's not just working for the mission but living
into it. Before you host a meal or plan a worship night, your team is
already becoming a recovery church community. If your team listens
well, loves one another, and reflects the kingdom—then you're already
forming the foundation of the community you are hoping to emerge.
So, start by becoming a community that shares life and practices grace
and let the experiments grow from that soil.

While planning meetings are important, so are occasional meals
or retreats together to deepen your bond. You should encounter each
other's stories and discover how God is working in one another's lives.
Pray with each other and for each other. Allow yourselves the space
to be playful and laugh together so that the mission is infused with
the joy of life with God and one another. When you let one another
down—an inevitable reality of working together with imperfect hu-
mans—practice asking for and extending forgiveness so that reconcili-
ation can flow in the midst of a community committed to grace and
truth.

The culture of the recovery church community will emerge from
the DNA of your team. So, make sure that the DNA you are setting
reflects the values and relational qualities that you hope to see.

Who needs to be invited to be part of the team?

What should be a regular part of your meetings to foster an
aligned, healthy team?

How will you deepen the bonds of your team?

God of New Beginnings,
You call us together not just to work, but to witness. We seek to
reflect your love in how we listen, serve, and dream side by side.
Make us a team rooted in grace and courageous in the small ex-
periments of faith. Let our differences become strength, our prayers
become vision, and our planning become worship. As we follow
the stirrings of your Spirit, may our life together become the first
expression of the healing you long to bring. In the name of Jesus we
pray, Amen.

Crafting the Table

Let each of you look not only to his own interests, but also to the interests of others.

— Philippians 2:4 (ESV)

After your good listening and discernment, it's time for your team to pick a starting point and start crafting a way forward, knowing that as you make some preliminary decisions and experiment, you will learn and iterate along the way.

One of the most frequent questions I (Roz) am asked about a Fresh Expression of Recovery is "what elements are included" in my recovery service? The question is like asking what should I put in a salad? The possibilities are endless. In the Picardo household, for sake of ease, I eat the same type of salad as my wife which contains spinach, craisins, goat cheese, apples, and her own blend of oil, vinegar and seasoning. I enjoy the salad but my affinity for salad when I am dining out is steak slices with blue cheese crumbles, and tomatoes over spinach. You get the point. Our affinity is much like our appetite as we prepare a meal for ourselves, but we should lean into awareness of what we might need to adjust when we are hosting others.

As we have touched on in previous chapters, Fresh Expressions should never be designed in a vacuum by one leader's ideas alone. Too often, what seems like a "great idea" to a church or leader doesn't actually meet the felt needs of the community. That's why we can't repeat enough that listening is essential: the shape of any emerging community must be guided by the context in which it takes root.

I experienced this firsthand while leading a church restart in a predominantly African American neighborhood. The church had been meeting in a nontraditional space, and although the signage indicated it was a faith community, many neighbors didn't recognize it as such. Before my time, a Saturday evening service had been launched, but it was mostly attended by commuters rather than local residents. When I began prayer walking, listening, and learning the culture of the neighborhood, it quickly became clear that a Saturday service felt unusual—even suspicious—to many in the community. Some wondered if we were even part of the Christian faith because we didn't gather on Sunday mornings.

As fall approached, we discerned it was time to make the transition to Sunday worship. I knew it would be painful for some of our Saturday night regulars, and it was—we lost a few. But those conversations and the listening process gave us confidence to move forward. When we launched on Sunday mornings, the response was immediate: our attendance tripled on the very first Sunday. More importantly, we were finally aligned with the rhythms and expectations of the people around us. That shift would never have happened if we hadn't slowed down, listened, and let the context shape our mission.

Let the Community Shape the Expression

When God nudges us to begin a Fresh Expression within the recovery community, it's essential that those who it is meant to serve are part of shaping it. This is about more than choosing worship elements; it's about cultivating ownership and community together. At my (Roz) church, Mosaic, we sensed God leading us to start Fighting Chance Recovery about four years into our ministry. By then, we had already partnered with recovery homes, and many in recovery were worshiping with us, getting baptized, experiencing transformation, serving, and finding belonging. It was miraculous to watch God raise up leaders from within this community. One woman, for example, began attending Sunday worship by bus after losing her license. She even joined our membership class via Zoom while commuting. None of us realized then that she would become one of the key servant leaders of Fighting Chance. As she grew in her healing journey, there was an inward calling she experienced to step out of her comfort zone and share her heart of recovery with others. Today, she is sober, thriving, a homeowner, and walking alongside others in their recovery journey. As we formed a team of those in recovery alongside others passionate about this work, we began praying, eating, and dreaming together. The shape of Fighting Chance Recovery emerged not from what we thought was best, but from listening to their longings and hopes for their peers. Accordingly, we suggest that you:

> Include those in recovery from the very start. Ask those in your circles who they know that should have a seat at the table.
>
> Build with, not for. Ownership builds when the work is shared among the people.
>
> Invest in emerging leaders. When God brings people on the team, find ways to invest and share responsibilities which creates a leadership pipeline.
>
> When we give room to a diversity of voices, the community is more likely to be appropriately shaped for the given context.

Experiment Early and Often

No matter what we imagine this new form of church was going to look like, experimentation is going to be key. In the church planting world I'm part of, we often held "preview services" before a public launch. These gatherings gave the community a taste of what worship was like and who we were as a church. I think of them as a kind of beta test—a chance to gather feedback, work out the bugs, and make improvements before going fully public. Just as beta testing is common in software, product design, and manufacturing, experiments let us refine both the experience and the community's sense of ownership.

To craft your own experiments helpful prompts to practice with a team can include:

"What if we tried this once?"

"I wonder what it would look like if we…?"

"Who needs to be at the table to run this idea by?"

"How will we know or recognize what worked?"

"What could make this meaningful and even fun?

For example, perhaps you have decided that you need to start with some simple community-building events to deepen your relationships among the residents of two local transition homes before developing some kind of worship service. Brainstorm as a team what it might look like to create an environment for deeper connection. Maybe one idea that rises to the top is a cookout and root beer float block party at the transition house. And the metric you're paying attention to is not "how many people attended," but rather, by the end of the event did we hear things like: "This was fun—we should do it again!" or "Do you need help grilling?" or "I'll scoop the ice cream." In other words, if we walk away with a sense of the community leaning in, then that tells us one thing. If we walk away with a feeling that we are still strangers, then we may need to try another kind of experiment.

Asking these kinds of questions will help your team take a nimble, open-handed approach to the mission. We are more likely to discover the places of resonance when we are willing to experiment, learn, and iterate in the direction most likely to connect with those God is inviting us to engage. Not only that, when we dare to ask questions like these aloud, don't be surprised that the Spirit often brings new insights to the surface.

Making Early Decisions

First, consider values that might be important for this mission. For example, one of the values we determined early on in our recovery community efforts was that we were going to be lay driven instead of clergy or staff driven; in other words; a recovery expression led by people in recovery for people in recovery. In fact, 99 percent of Fighting Chance is completely lay-led.

Let me give you a window in some of the values that rose to the top for us:

Leadership

Lay-driven instead of clergy or staff driven

Therefore, until there was a team of committed lay servants, we would not be ready to move forward.

A recovery expression led by people in recovery for people in recovery

Therefore, until those in recovery were willing to step into leadership roles, we were not yet where we needed to be.

Music

Music has the unique capacity to tap into and open up the soul and open people to the presence of God.

Therefore, music would need to be part of the gatherings.

The style of music should be resonant for the recovery community.

Therefore, the Mosaic band couldn't just show up to Fighting Chance and play the prior Sunday's band play-list. The music for this community would need to lean more heavily into familiar rock music rather than all gospel-oriented music.

The music leadership should include those at the heart of this mission.

Accordingly, a new band formed—some part of the Mosaic Church music team, but others from the recovery community leading with their gifts of music.

Serenity Prayer

The Serenity Prayer is a familiar "liturgy" for the 12-step community and would be a natural bridge of invitation into a journey of intention, surrender, and trust in the Living God.

This prayer quickly became a core element of our gatherings. Composed by theologian Reinhold Niebuhr in the 1930s to prepare soldiers for battle, in the recovery space, this prayer has become a communal battle cry for those fighting to overcome addiction. While many newcomers would not be able to recite the Lord's Prayer from memory, almost all could say the Serenity Prayer. This gave our community a shared liturgy and a shared intention.

As you can see, each values-based decision we made had implications for how we would move forward. It is through this process, and the underlying values, that other elements found their place in the rhythms of Fighting Chance Recovery.

Celebrating Progress: Clean-Time Shoutouts

One of my personal favorite elements that our team dreamed up is a time in our gathering (slotted after the Serenity Prayer) that we call, "Clean-Time Shoutouts."

How It Works

Individuals will shout aloud how many days, weeks, months or years that have been sober from all mind-altering substances, compulsions or behaviors.

After each shoutout, there is an eruption of applause, whether that person has a few days of sobriety or many years under their belt.

What We Celebrate

    Milestones of sobriety at every stage
    Regaining custody of children
    Gaining employment or housing
    Paying off fines
    Getting married
    Graduating from a program or school
    Reconnecting with loved ones.

Through this rhythm of sharing, we get a front row seat to the miracles that are taking place in people's lives.

The Message at the Center

We have also developed a rotation for the "meat" of our gathering with:

Lead Stories: testimonies of transformation

Step Study: a deep dive into one of the 12 Steps

Panel Conversations: peer-led stories (Testimonies of Transformation) are encouraging and powerful examples to others that recovery is possible. Each story is vetted and only those who have at least a year of sobriety are invited to share. We work with these story-sharers in advance, helping them shape their story and refine the length. We encourage people to make Jesus the hero of their testimony, not simply to dwell on their darkest days, highlighting the transformation the Lord has brought. At times, we also offer a gentle warning before certain stories, as we have found that the details may be triggering for those who carry their own trauma.

Step by Step: Teaching Through the 12 Steps reflects our rhythm of covering one of the steps in greater detail each month. We strongly advocate for the steps originated by Alcoholics Anonymous and bring biblical teaching to each one. Within the scope of a year, we will have covered them all: 12 Steps in 12 months.

Raw and Real: panel conversations allow participants to hear from peers wrestling with real-life issues. Panel members represent both men and women at different stages of recovery, and cover topics such as coping with the holidays, handling relationships, navigating relapse triggers, or managing everyday emotions. A moderator prepares questions in advance and shares them with panel members. It can feel risky and raw—you never quite know what someone might say—but we believe the honesty and authenticity it brings are worth it.

Ending with Encouragement and Prayer

We always end our time together by pointing people to:

Next Steps: Get into some sort of recovery group, get a sponsor that can help them navigate their recovery journey, become a sponsor themselves, and get a spiritual mentor who can walk beside them on their new spiritual life.

Ministry Time: We end our gatherings by offering prayer for anyone who needs it.

These elements at Fighting Chance Recovery were not stumbled upon by accident but bathed in prayer and ideated by a team of passionate folks who are not only fighting for their own recovery but the recovery of others.

Discernment Through Dialogue

As you begin to dream and contemplate what a Fresh Expression of Recovery can look like, pray and ask who else needs to have a seat at the table, and practice the art of listening after asking some thoughtful questions. Gather what you are learning and begin to have thoughtful dialogue that can lead into experimentation.

After each conversation, reflect on these questions:

In what ways am I inviting others into leadership rather than creating something on my own?

What values do we sense are important for this emerging community?

What elements that were described in this chapter resonate with your team and which ones don't?

What other elements might be important in your context?

*God of Wisdom, we humbly ask you for the discernment, knowl-
edge, wisdom, and understanding to make Spirit-led decisions
when it comes to the community you want to shape, not about our
preferences but the new thing you want to create in our midst. Give
us guidance and vision of what you want to shape with the people
you are calling to be part of the community. In Jesus' name, Amen.*

Chapter 6

Pick Your Path

Commit your work to the LORD, and your plans will be established.
—Proverbs 16:3 (ESV)

Every September, Apple fans gather—both in person and online—for the highly anticipated Keynote event. It's when Apple unveils the latest iPhones, Apple watches, and other products with major updates. More than a product showcase, the event sets the tone for the year ahead. Each release reflects years of research into how people live, work, and connect. Apple doesn't roll out features randomly; they intentionally design products that meet real needs.

Now, before you remind me that the Christian faith isn't an industry catering to consumers—hear me out. Apple's approach illustrates something churches often miss. They spend countless hours studying what people long for and then build products with those people in mind. In contrast, many churches begin with the community in view, but over time drift inward. Ministries that once met real needs slowly become shaped by the preferences of boards, committees, or default leaders. The result? Their purpose fades, and participation shrinks to a small circle of insiders.

Why Models Matter

Most mission initiatives that have emerged in different contexts have some patterns that others look to for guidance. We often refer to these as "models." Models reflect the felt-needs, values, and rhythms of the people we are called to serve. Models set the tone and theological orientation of a given ministry. They determine how accessible and replicable the approach is for a ministry. It impacts how we train leaders, the materials we use, the servant teams' expectations, and the long-term sustainability of a ministry. Our models should not serve ourselves. They are simply a tool and a vehicle to share God's love with our communities and world.

Three Primary Models for Recovery Ministry

When we talk about models, we are referring to faith-based worship and community, built on the foundation of Jesus. While Alcoholics Anonymous (AA) and the different spin-offs associated with various addictions, i.e., Sexaholics Anonymous (SA), Narcotics Anonymous (NA) etc. have widespread name recognition and encourage the participants to seek a Higher Power throughout their meeting format, faith-based recovery worshipping communities unapologetically encourage people to consider naming Jesus as their higher power. However, it is not a prerequisite to attend.

One of the most common questions I get from leaders and teams who feel called to start a Fresh Expression of Recovery is what type of model they should use. The quick answer is that the best model is the one that fits their context. There are no bad models, but ones that simply fit better than others. There is not a one-size-fits-all approach.

Celebrate Recovery (CR) Model[1]

One of the most recognized models in recovery ministry is Saddleback's Celebrate Recovery (CR). Celebrate Recovery was founded in 1991 by John Baker and Pastor Rick Warren. Founded in 1991, John Baker who was himself in recovery, approached Warren with the idea of starting a Christ-centered 12-step program rooted in Jesus'

---

1. https://cr-files.s3.amazonaws.com/AWS+-+DNA+OF+CELEBRATE+RECOVERY+(3).pdf

Beatitudes from the Sermon on the Mount. With Warren's support, Celebrate Recovery was launched at Saddleback and quickly grew into a worldwide movement, bearing fruit in thousands of churches.

There are some strengths to using this model:

Strong brand recognition: It has become so widely popular that many in Christian circles are familiar with it.

Ready-made resources: Saddleback has also developed extensive resources, making it easy for a team to launch Celebrate Recovery without reinventing the wheel. The kit includes everything you need and countless examples of thriving Celebrate Recovery ministries across the country provide a model to follow.

For Fresh Expressions that are just getting started—or those looking for a plug-and-play framework—Celebrate Recovery can be a strong fit. Teams considering it should visit a local Celebrate Recovery in your area to get a feel for the format, and training opportunities are available through regional and national conferences.

But there are some challenges to this model that you need to be aware of:

Inflexibility: Using the Celebrate Recovery brand and materials requires signing a covenant agreement and committing to follow the core DNA of the program. This means you cannot blend Celebrate Recovery content with other recovery models, and the curriculum, teaching, and format cannot be modified when using the Celebrate Recovery branding.

Theological Misalignment Potential: The rigidity of Celebrate Recovery can present a level of challenges depending on your context. For example, churches may not line up with Celebrate Recovery from a theological perspective, especially if they are not rooted in an evangelical stream. Also, where church harm has been pervasive, a community could be leery of branding that potentially triggers someone or be perceived as institutional control.

Length: On a practical level, because Celebrate Recovery includes multiple components—such as an optional meal beforehand and the Solid Rock Café fellowship time afterward—a full gathering can last between two and one-half to three hours.

Celebrate Recovery can be an incredible resource and has reached thousands of people but can also be a contextual and theological mismatch. The real question is not if Celebrate Recovery is good or bad but is it the right tool to reach your identified community?

Custom Model

For teams exploring alternatives, many churches have found a custom model to be more effective. At Mosaic Church, our Fighting Chance Recovery Community is one example. Our team, broadly familiar with the 12-step community, multicultural in our approach, and full of ideas, developed our rhythms and practices from the ground up. The strength of the custom model:

Flexibility, it can be fully shaped around the team, the context, and the people you feel called to reach.

Teams set the rhythm, frequency, elements, and activities.

You are not bound to someone else's recipe.

It is the opposite of the one size fits all approach.

That freedom, however, comes with challenges.

No handbook means an initial heavy lift to organize training and equip leaders.

Developing a custom plan and preparing a team can take
significant time.

Risk of drifting into ambiguity by making constant
changes without a clear vision.

Without discipline, a custom model can feel unstable, as
gatherings either try to include too much or too little.

The key is balancing creativity with clarity, ensuring changes
emerge from a healthy feedback loop rather than from guesswork.

Hybrid Model

A third option could be a hybrid model. In this scenario, you
may research many different recovery ministries being offered in different contexts, applying some of what you've seen elsewhere in your
own setting, while rejecting others because they may not be the best
fit for your context. You might learn from our practices at Fighting Chance (which we freely share with others in case it could be
helpful for their setting or can catalyze further ideas), while finding
inspiration from other settings as well. These exposures give your
team options to consider and space to innovate. What will emerge
is a hybrid: something that doesn't look exactly what you've seen in
other places yet draws on some of the experience of other ministries.

The Strengths:

Incorporates only those aspects from other models/
examples that fit the context

Provides a balance of learning from others and creative license

Makes team more adaptable when modifications need to take place since they do not need to "color inside the lines" of someone else's curriculum.

Can be a fit for experienced teams and individuals with recovery ministry backgrounds

The bottom line is the hybrid approach could work well when the Fresh Expression has a clear identity of who they are and what God is calling them to become. There is enough experience that the team does not require a proscriptive course, but enough humility to recognize that they would benefit from drawing from some experience from other ministries that are further down the road and have more expertise in the recovery arena.

The hybrid model also has its own set of considerations and challenges.

The Weaknesses:

Can create complexity in coordination as you cobble many different ideas and components into a coherent whole.

Scattered efforts can lead to confusion and an inconsistent structure if not enough attention is given to organization and value-centered decision making. Even the best ideas from other models will be ineffective in your setting if they don't make sense for your local context or intentionally embody the values of your local mission.

Mixing multiple models can be unsettling for those in recovery if there is no consistency or it appears haphazard.

And, without ready-made resources, perhaps one of the most important considerations is how you will train a team and leaders to be equipped to live out the vision. Organized and equipped leadership is key to an effective mission, so in these custom or hybrid approaches, you must tackle some form of training process or risk crippling your mission with misaligned or disorganized leadership.

Discerning the Right Fit for Your Context

As I tell my congregation when preaching, don't take my word for it, but read the scriptures for yourself, I offer the exact word of caution when it comes to recovery models. Do your own research and do not rely on the few examples I listed, because it is not a comprehensive list. Only you and your team—through prayerful discernment, conversations with the greater community, and deep listening--can determine which model is the best fit for your context.

Questions for Discernment

If you are trying to determine what model is the contextual fit for your Recovery Fresh Expression, here are a few reflection questions:

1. What is your team's experience level?

    a. How many of them are new to recovery, where are they in the faith journey, and what is their experience, if any, in any type of faith-based recovery ministry or program?

2. What theological convictions or spiritual values must shape the model you choose? These are your non-negotiables.

    For example, it could be that your group values include:

    a. belief in second chances,

    b. a posture that recovery is a journey and not just a class to take,

    c. an acknowledgement that recovery is more than behavior modification but rather a deep spiritual and emotional healing that needs to take place.

At Fighting Chance Recovery, one of our non-negotiable values is safety: we believe that safe processes create safe people and safe places. Because people in recovery are in a vulnerable state, we knew that we would need to be vigilant to create safe space, including a mindfulness that not everyone involved in the ministry will be in a state of mind to prioritize safety and thus our processes must provide the healthy guardrails.

3. How much structure do your leaders and community members need?

   Pay attention to what model is most resonant for your team, their familiarity with the recovery space, and the needs of the community. For example, if you have ample volunteers but they have little experience with the recovery process, Celebrate Recovery could be a good fit because it lays out every dimension of recovery ministry in painstaking detail. A custom model could make sense for your team if you have experienced individuals with a strong creative bent committed to the mission. A hybrid approach might be most helpful where the team would benefit from exposure to a wide variety of options before applying elements they have encountered into a contextual fit for their local setting.

4. And not to seem repetitive but are there people in recovery and from the community helping shape the model?

   a. Many times, leaders and teams are making decisions based on their preferences without the study, research, and community listening needed to make Spirit-led decisions. The best leaders and team members could be the ones who are not currently in your network but are a prayer away.

Hold the Model Loosely, Hold the Mission Firmly

Whatever model you and your team determine is the best contextual fit, a feedback loop becomes invaluable throughout the life your Fresh Expression community. Think of ways to continue to have conversations, formal and informal, with the people who are directly participating, but also with those you are hoping to reach. It requires a fine balance of being faithful to the model and a willingness to be flexible. At the end of the day, a well-chosen model is only a tool. The model will not do the work for you. Do not grasp so tightly to the structure that it no longer serves the people you are trying to engage or the faith community that is emerging. Be prayerful, ask questions, listen deeply, and incorporate the people that God has placed around you.

After each conversation, reflect on these questions:

After considering the discernment questions around the models, what direction is a good fit for your context and why?

What non-negotiable theological or spiritual values have emerged as you think about your community?

What voices from the recovery community are we incorporating at this stage? What are we hearing and how does that hone the direction we need to take?

Gracious God, we come to you with listening ears and humble hearts as we discern what steps are needed to find the right fit for our context. As much as we love the new thing you want to do, we know you love those we are seeking to gather more than we could ever imagine. Guide the right voices into the conversations and the team members you want to empower to lead this new work that we would live into your preferred future. In Jesus' name, Amen.

Chapter 7

Good News in the Midst of Recovery

*My only aim is to finish the race and complete the task the Lord Jesus
has given me—the task of testifying to the good news of God's grace.*

—*Acts 20:24*

A model is only a framework. But it is the gospel that gives life.
How will we both embody and proclaim the gospel in this
ministry? Perhaps we can look to Jesus' example. As Jesus was going
about his ministry, he told different parables in different situations,
seeking to reveal life in the kingdom of God through language and
metaphors, as well as signs and wonders, that were intended for different
audiences.

Part of contextualizing the gospel among a particular community
is asking: what aspects of the gospel might feel most like good
news here? Depending on what Christian tradition we come from,
we may be used to talking about Jesus in one way: "Jesus died for our
sins" or "Jesus came to seek the lost." But there are many dimensions
to Jesus' ministry. Yes, he died for our sins and came to seek the lost.
But he also came to set the captive free and eat with sinners and
clasp the hands of the unclean. He came to bring life out of death
and weep with those who mourn. In other words, there are countless
ways to connect people to the good news of Jesus.

That's important to recognize in a Fresh Expression of Recovery. When you can be attuned to places of spiritual openness, it can point you to the kinds of spiritual dialogue that might be most impactful.

You see, addiction is never just about substances or behaviors. Rather, it's about a deep ache, a longing, or a desperate search for something to make life bearable. Recovery is the courageous, ongoing journey of unearthing that ache and seeking healing. What people in that process don't need is a brochure about Jesus; they need a loving Jesus-shaped community to help them discover the profound good news that they are invited into.

Along those lines, certain aspects of Jesus' life and message tend to be particularly resonant in the recovery journey. Let's explore a few of them.

1. Jesus Meets Us in Our Powerlessness

    One of the first steps of recovery is admitting powerlessness—that life has become unmanageable. The gospel meets this head-on. Jesus doesn't come for the self-sufficient; he comes for those who know they cannot save themselves. His words, "Blessed are the poor in spirit" (Matthew 5:3), speak directly to the one who has hit rock bottom. The very place of weakness is where God's grace meets us most powerfully. And we are all poor without Jesus.

2. Jesus Offers a New Identity

    Shame is a constant companion in addiction. Guilt is the sense that I did bad, but shame shapes an identity that I am bad. Therefore, many in recovery carry labels—failure, addict, screw-up—that weigh them down. The gospel offers a new identity: beloved child of God, forgiven, renewed, set free. Jesus doesn't gloss over past wounds, but he reframes them within the larger story of redemption. This is why testimonies in recovery spaces are so powerful—they echo the biblical refrain: "I was… but now, in Christ, I am…" A Fresh Eexpression of Recovery can help nurture practices of naming and reclaiming this new identity in Christ.

3. Jesus Creates a Community of Belonging

   Addiction isolates: recovery restores connection. Jesus' ministry was filled with stories of restoration into community: from the leper whose hand Jesus touched to heal him back into community to the prodigal son who had screwed up and was welcomed back into the family. Jesus consistently formed communities where tax collectors ate with fishermen, and sinners dined with saints. The kind of community we are seeking to develop incarnates this same heartbeat, and the Jesus who restores is the companion who invites those who were once isolated into a fellowship of belonging.

4. Jesus Brings Healing and Wholeness

   Recovery is not simply about avoiding relapse; it's about finding a deeper wholeness. It is not merely behavior modification but healing from the inside out. Jesus is the great healer, and he confronts each of us with the same question that he asked a paralyzed man in Scripture: "Do you want to be well?" (John 5:6 NCV). For the person weary from relapse or weighed down by their past, that question is at the same time both deeply unsettling and deeply hopeful. Leaders can be attentive to the ways Jesus is already stirring desires for healing and walk gently with people toward that wholeness.

5. Jesus Redeems Suffering into Purpose

   Recovery is rarely linear or tidy. Setbacks happen. Pain lingers. But the gospel proclaims a God who wastes nothing. Even scars become part of the story God uses to bring hope to others. The Apostle Paul speaks of boasting in weakness so that Christ's power may be revealed (2 Corinthians 12:9). In recovery, wounds often become the most powerful witness—proof that grace is real. Your team can help create space where stories of struggle are honored as testimonies of God's ongoing work of redemption. Or as Fighting Chance often inspires: "Your mess can become your message."

6. Jesus Practices Radical Honesty

   In recovery, honesty is the bedrock—telling the truth about yourself, your past, your weakness. Jesus modeled this same unflinching truth-telling. He calls out hypocrisy and sin, yet in the same breath extends mercy. For people who are weary of masks and pretending, Jesus' radical authenticity feels like fresh air.

7. Jesus Welcomes the Outcast

   Addiction often pushes people to the margins. Some become estranged from family; others feel stigmatized by society. Jesus consistently moves toward those the world avoids: lepers, prostitutes, tax collectors. His table is set for the ones others have written off. For people in recovery, this welcome is deeply healing—it affirms their worth and dismantles shame. Radical acceptance with contagious goodness leads to transformation.

8. Jesus Invites Daily Dependence

   Recovery is a "one day at a time" journey. Jesus echoes this in the Lord's Prayer: "Give us this day our daily bread" (Matthew 6:11 ESV) He invites followers not to carry tomorrow's burden but to trust God's provision moment by moment. Those who are taking each day sober know they need more than their own willpower. Jesus offers them himself, and invites them to lean into God's promises, God's provision, and God's strength.

9. Jesus Offers Rest for the Weary

Many in recovery are bone-tired—tired of striving, of failing, of starting over. Jesus' invitation, "Come to me, all you who are weary and burdened, and I will give you rest" (Matthew 11:28), speaks directly to the exhausted soul. Jesus doesn't demand performance, but offers rest, gentleness, and lightness. Or as Eugene Peterson translates this verse in the Message, "Get away with me and you'll recover your life." (Matthew 11:28 MSG)

10. Jesus Walks the Road of Suffering

Recovery involves facing trauma, grief, and pain head-on. Jesus does not avoid suffering—he walks straight into it, carrying the cross. He knows betrayal, abandonment, physical agony, and despair. For those in recovery, this is powerful: Jesus is not distant from their suffering but has walked through it himself and promises resurrection on the other side.

Exploring These Themes in the Life of Community

How might spiritual conversations show up in your Fresh Expression of Recovery? Think beyond the pulpit and the sermon. Sometimes they take the form of a short teaching with follow up small group conversations. Sometimes they happen in informal conversation around shared meals or firepits. Sometimes they happen in more formalized mentorship relationships. Sometimes they happen in organic conversations before or after a gathering. Sometimes they happen as you work alongside one another to set up chairs or scoop ice cream.

Your team will likely be organizing and planning some form of worship gathering but recognize that some of the most profound faith exploration will happen alongside your plans, in the organic conversations and the unexpected moments. You will want to be primed for when those holy moments present themselves.

In addition, if you want to walk alongside recovery communities in meaningful ways, there are some appropriate postures to keep in mind.

Learn to listen without fixing. We need to resist the urge to offer quick answers and instead embody the patient, non-anxious presence of Christ. Don't preach at people. Accompany them and let their curiosity open the doors to deeper conversation.

Normalize weakness. Effective spiritual companionship calls us to lean into your own vulnerability. People need to see our imperfections so they can discover that faith is not about perfection but dependence on grace.

Respect the recovery journey. Many in recovery find the 12 Steps profoundly spiritual. Learn the language and rhythms of recovery so you can honor and connect gospel themes with lived experience.

Focus on belonging before belief. Recovery communities thrive on unconditional acceptance. Your Fresh Expression community can mirror this by making space for people to belong long before they feel ready to believe.

Prepare for holy interruptions. Moments of breakthrough often come unexpectedly—in the middle of a relapse, a group meeting, or a late-night phone call. Your team should cultivate a prayerful attentiveness that is ready to notice and name God's presence in these moments.

Ask:

Where do I see some of the spiritual themes in this chapter in my own life, and how might that shape the way I walk alongside those in recovery?

What aspects of the good news of Jesus would I add to this list that might particularly resonate with those navigating recovery?

How comfortable am I with my own weakness and vulnerability?

In what ways could modeling that be a gift to those navigating recovery?

Jesus,
Rekindle in us the joy of your good news.
Help us to bear witness to your goodness as we trust in you to open
hearts...
Give us courage to be honest, grace to be gentle,
and wisdom to notice the holy moments of breakthrough.
May our lives bear witness to your mercy,
and may a new community of hope and belonging
take root through the power of your Spirit.
Amen.

Chapter 8

Consider Additional Elements

Rejoice with those who rejoice; mourn with those who mourn.
—Romans 12:15

When we envision a recovery church community, the worship gathering is often the centerpiece. It's where stories are shared, grace is proclaimed, and Christ is encountered in powerful ways. But for many people in recovery, one service a week isn't enough. In fact, if we want to create communities that are truly healing, we will need think beyond the service. We have to ask:

What other spaces, rhythms, and supports could help people stay connected, grounded, and growing in their recovery and faith?

Creating Holistic Support in a Recovery Church Community

Perhaps you will want to consider a few additions that might help your Recovery Church become more than a gathering and more like a true spiritual home.

A Pre-Service Meal

Sharing a simple meal before worship can break down barriers, build trust, and create space for authentic relationships. For many people in recovery, especially those rebuilding community or routines, having a place to belong before the service begins makes a huge difference.

- Practical Tips:

    - Keep it simple: chili and cornbread, soup and sand-wiches, tacos. Or consider having participants bring a dish to share. You don't have to do it all for people. After all, this is community!

    - Involve volunteers from both inside and outside the recovery community.

    - Create a shared "table culture": inclusive, respectful, and open to all.

    - Consider some table questions that can foster conversation and connection with one another. The meal is often where people feel safe enough to return. Long before they trust Jesus, they trust the food and the welcome.

Childcare that Builds Trust

Many people navigating recovery are also parenting—sometimes while doing the hard work of healing rela-tionships with their children. Offering childcare during worship is a practical act of grace that makes it possible for parents to show up, breathe, and receive.

- Practical Tips:

    - Make sure all volunteers have background checks and basic training in child protection.

    - Create a warm, calm, and trauma-informed environ-ment for children.

    - Offer simple crafts, stories, or music that mirror the

healing themes of the service.

– Don't treat it as babysitting—treat it as ministry. When a mom in early recovery knows her toddler is safe and loved, she can finally relax enough to receive what God wants to give her.

Ongoing Weekly Support

One hour a week isn't enough to hold a life together. Many recovery church communities have found that offering additional touchpoints during the week helps people stay grounded, grow spiritually, and develop life skills for long-term transformation. These might include:

- Peer-Led Support Groups: Small, trusted circles where people can share openly without fear of judgment. These can be 12-step recovery groups or specific groups shaped around particular needs (grief, relapse prevention, trauma recovery, etc.).

- Bible Studies or Faith Conversations: Keep them honest and real. No pressure to have all the answers. Just create space to listen, learn, and grow together.

- Workshops or Classes: Offer practical skills like budgeting, resume writing, parenting, cooking, or healthy relationships. These support recovery in real-life ways.

- Mentorship or Discipleship Pairs: Consider inviting people into intentional, relational growth with others just a step or two ahead on the journey.

Organically Developing Small Groups

Recognize that sometimes shared commonalities or natural relationships are signs that there is group of people ready to be launched into a small group. They might be in the same season of life or live in the same neighborhood. Perhaps they are all at a similar point in the recovery journey or they all like to work out at the gym.

Tears were the starting point for one small group. One father was attending a worship gathering struggling to hold it together, but a few stray tears signaled his pain. A couple sitting nearby reached out with compassion. In that exchange, they discovered both of them were navigating rocky relationships with impulsive, substance-abusing teenagers. The couple suggested they meet for coffee on Thursday night to connect and share stories.

The following week, they ran into another kindred heartbroken parent and invited her to coffee. What began with one simple cup of coffee one Thursday night grew to a small group of parents negotiating their own recovery while navigating the complexity of parenting rebellious teenagers. That group became a lifeline. They opened Scripture together, held space for the pain, prayed for one another, and shared honestly about setbacks, victories, and everything in between.

Where you see the potential for small groups to emerge, name it, celebrate it, and invite people to take that step together.

A Worshiping Community Is Just the Beginning

If the worship service is the entry point, these other supports are the scaffolding. They help people hold their lives together and experience God's love not just once a week—but in the everyday.

Don't worry about building it all at once.

And remember: sometimes, the most meaningful support emerges from organic, relational spaces that were not part of the strategic plan. Who would have guessed that a small group would emerge from the group of parents navigating the teenage years? Pay attention to the surprising way God might be at work and find ways to build on what God is already doing.

Ask:

What is most needed right now?

What is God stirring in our team?

What could we try, even on a small scale?

What additional element might your team need to consider at this stage of the mission and why?

What would be needed to bring that element to life?

How could you start bringing those dreams and needs before the Lord?

God of healing and wholeness,
you are not confined to one hour of worship. You meet us in meals,
in small groups, in shared stories, in laughter over coffee, and quiet
prayers in difficult times. Help us build a community that reflects
your love in every corner. Show us where extra support is needed.
Stir in us the creativity to respond where you lead. Let every meal,
every group, every act of welcome be a doorway to your presence. In
the name of Jesus, we pray. Amen.

Where Vision Meets Reality

Suppose one of you wants to build a tower. Won't you first sit down and estimate the cost...?

— Luke 14:28

I despise the saying, "The Devil is in the details" because I believe God is in the details (and the Devil tries to mess with them!). If you are not a detail or logistic person, find or recruit those on the team who are. Admittedly, I (Roz) am more of a visionary and less inclined to thinking through every step needed to live into the vision. I have seen ministries with lots of energy and passion but little organization. Conversely, I have seen ministries which are overly organized but have little passion for what they are doing. The details, logistics, and systems are simply a conduit to help the vision of a recovery faith community come to fruition.

The considerations laid out here are ones my teams, as well as countless other recovery ministries, have wrestled through. It is not meant to be an exhaustive list, but these are key matters we encounter when coaching and advising other teams. As a reminder, throughout this book you have heard that your context will be the deciding factor, and that is the case in these matters as well. Our goal is to share some of the learnings from other settings and then let you decide what best fits your own setting.

Planning The Environment

The first practical consideration is space. Space is arbitrary, yet space is everything. You will often hear people say, "space doesn't matter" or "you can meet anywhere," both of which are true to an extent. But there is a psychology of space that plays a role in how people perceive an environment and gathering.

In my first church plant, we met in a historic downtown movie theater. The launch was invigorating, seeing nine months of work culminate into a community of gathered people experiencing life together. But nobody warned me about post-launch. There was natural attrition in our second week for which I was unprepared. What made matters worse was that the movie theater auditorium swallowed us up because it was too big. When there is not enough critical mass to somewhat fill a space, first-time visitors question if they are in the right place or if this is a gathering they want to attend. As one of my friends asks, "How likely are you to stop at a new restaurant if the parking lot appears empty at 6 p.m. on a Friday evening." The opposite is true when a space is overcrowded and there is no room in the inn! It can feel inhospitable when people are packed close together and there is not enough seat distancing for a visitor navigating a room full of strangers.

When thinking of space, location matters.

Is it visible or will people walk or drive right by it without even realizing it?

Is it handicap accessible?

Is it non-threatening?

Sometimes the best space for any Fresh Expression might be outside the four walls of a traditional church facility. If hoping to engage those who are de-churched or unchurched, the church building may carry a stigma that is hard to shake. However, don't just make assumptions, because for those in recovery, some may feel surprisingly comfortable in a church building because so many of their addiction recovery meetings are in the basement of a church.

If your team is discerning that a church-neutral place is best, then it means you will need to find your "persons of peace" who would be willing to allow you in their café, restaurant, or place of business. What are persons of peace? In Luke 10, Jesus teaches that as his disciples are sent into homes, businesses, and communities, we are to share peace with those we encounter. There will be some who share peace, and when that happens, it is a sign that we are in a scenario that is ripe for the gospel to take root.

In practical terms, persons of peace do not have belong to a faith community or even be a Christian, but they resonate with the vision you share with them. Often, they are trusted and networked among the community with which you are seeking to connect, and they can often open doors for your ministry that you can't open for yourself. Whether that's sharing their facility or resources or simply serving as a bridge of relationship among the community, introducing you to their friends and networks and thereby legitimizing you as a someone who can be trusted. For example, as one of the leaders at Fighting Chance felt a burden to start an additional recovery gathering on a different night of the week, she began to recognize that God was providing a person of peace. She had developed a relationship with a key individual in a local treatment and vocational center. As she shared her dream of a faith community closer to the center of gravity of recovery, this treatment center insider shared her enthusiasm, offering the center's event space—including the stage, seating, and kitchen—for the gatherings to take place. Simultaneously, God was raising up potential participants and a team through this leader's growing relationships, not only among her existing networks but among those who were being connected with her through this person of peace. Thursday Night Live kicked off in that treatment and vocational center, quickly growing to over one hundred participants a week.

What else might you need to consider? Depending on your model you may or may not need access to audio-visual equipment, storage for equipment, or space for meals and childcare. Also, be aware that it is not uncommon to start off in one space and move as the needs of the Fresh Expression develop and grow. Stay nimble, open, and discerning to what could be next.

The Power of Rhythm and Routine

Perhaps the location question is simple for your team to negotiate, but the question of timing and frequency (how often you meet) may feel more complicated. Again, there are no right or wrong answers.

Will you meet weekly? Bi-monthly? Monthly?

Evening or daytime?

Weekday or weekend?

Everything as one group, or sometimes in multiple smaller groups?

I know of some gatherings that meet monthly and others that meet weekly. Those considerations will depend on conversations with your team, their bandwidth, conversations with the greater community, and discovering when might be the most optimal time. Researching people's work-life patterns and availability is crucial. Before Fighting Chance Recovery settled on Wednesday evenings we researched when other faith-based recovery meetings were taking place because we wanted to fill a need where there was a void. But for your setting, Wednesday could be the one night of the week that has the best attended AA meeting, and you recognize it would not be wise to "compete" with what already exists. Context will need to drive these decisions.

Removing Barriers to Belonging

In the prior chapter, we looked at the possibility of adding the elements of a shared meal or childcare. These may make strategic sense for your emerging community, but they also add to the complexity of the operation. You will have to enter into these elements with eyes open.

Shared Meal
_____

When it comes to a shared meal, food is God's love language and something beautiful can happen around the table. Many find that a meal before or a café time after is great for relationship building. However, it is important to recognize that it takes a whole team to tackle the logistics, which include:

Meal planning

Food preparation schedule

Responding to dietary needs

Clean-up

Cost

Health department regulations

That translates into both monetary and human resources. Where meals have been effectively incorporated, there are often separate teams that take on the meal aspect of the mission in order to prevent volunteer burnout. The difficult part is recruiting more volunteers. Have your team press into their networks because there are people who want to give back that are passionate about cooking and thrive in behind-the-scenes serving opportunities. One doesn't need to be in recovery to serve, anyone is welcome, and it widens the circle.

Childcare

If you are considering adding childcare to the mix, the same strategy applies. While it can be helpful removing the barriers of dinner and childcare for people getting off work and wanting to come to a Fresh Expression Recovery gathering, it adds to the checklist of logistics needed. Much like the meal element, to pull off well-managed childcare, it takes a separate volunteer team that is:

Background-checked

Trained

Able to create a safe space to receive children.

Meals and childcare can be powerful ways of removing barriers for families and single parents who want to participate more fully in a recovery community.

Invitation as Relationships

One thing vital for any vibrant fresh expression is relationship-building. The team can find recovery homes, programs, and ministries with which to connect. Often those organizations are looking for mentors, people who can teach basic life skills classes, and even Bible studies. Go and volunteer and encourage those on your team to do the same. The art of invitation will rise naturally as relationships are built.

Prioritize Relationships Over Promotions

You might have a billboard proclaiming you are the most welcoming group in your area, but it will be incongruent if new people show up, are not welcomed, acknowledged, or spoken to. Hear me out, I am not saying advertisements, social media, branding, and logos are inherently evil, but they are simply tools for the primary mission of loving people in the way of Jesus. We cannot become so reliant on the tools that we neglect personal invitations.

Build friendships, word of mouth, and organic connections.

No one wants to be a marketing target.

Advertising and branding can mislead if they do not match people's experience of you.

From "For" to "With"

Finally, there is a philosophical shift to think about when it comes to recovery. It is imperative to eliminate the us and them mindset. The first step in a shared ministry is creating rhythms of ongoing listening with an intentional feedback loop. It is not just a ministry for others; we are inviting people to be in ministry with us. We want the community to help shape the ministry, improve and adjust as needed, and to take an active role of participation and leadership. When spectators become participants, they discover their dignity and worth as co-creators in the community.

How do we quickly get people involved? By cultivating a culture and environment in which people can encounter Jesus, experience community, and find a meaningful place to serve alongside. There is no insignificant task when it comes to setting up chairs, preparing a meal, providing childcare, or running tech.

Details Matter

When we pay attention to the details and logistics, we are intentionally caring for others and fostering hospitality in every part of a person's experience. Welcome others and be an ever-expanding circle of God's grace. Plan well. Stay flexible. And trust that God is in the details.

After each conversation, reflect on these questions:

What practical needs (space, schedule, meal, childcare) do I need to plan for in our Fresh Expressions Recovery?

How might I shift from an "us and them" mindset to true community co-creation?

Is there any detail that you and your team can investigate to help people feel seen, welcomed, heard, and valued?

Gracious God, we come to you in gratitude for caring about the details more than we ever could. Help us move from being a solo heroic leader than needs to do it on our own to equipping and empowering those around us who you have gifted and called to the work. We pray for those divine appointments and conversations that will come with those persons of peace, and those you are calling to be part of this community. In Jesus' name, Amen.

What we can communicate is that you matter.
You belong.
You can be part of something bigger than yourself.

Chapter 10

Fueling the Vision

*And my God will meet all your needs according to the riches of his
glory in Christ Jesus.*

— Philippians 4:19

T here are not many people I know who engage in ministry because they want to manage budgets or make giving appeals or
ask for in-kind donations. Ministry training and seminaries do very
little in preparing leaders for the necessary and practical component
of funding ministry. The financial aspects of funding ministry can
be overwhelming, perhaps even frightening. But what if we shifted
our perspective from fundraising to fueling the mission? If we want
to power a vision for a recovery church community, we will likely
need fuel.

Budgeting for the Mission

Ministry planning involves budgeting, and we must count the
cost. So, you would be wise to map out a realistic financial projection.
Try to come up with real numbers—don't just make something up.

The cost will include both one-time start-up expenses and the
ongoing expenses to fuel the ministry year after year.

One-time expenses may include:

Preparing the physical environment: painting, physical preparation to make the space more hospitable, chairs, round tables, signage, etc. If you are in a third space, you may need very little for venue preparation.

Audio-visual equipment: microphones, speakers, mixer board, projector or flat screen, laptop, etc. You don't need the latest and greatest equipment. There are perhaps churches that are looking to bless your efforts and would be willing to give away some of those items or sell them at a reduced rate.

Curriculum (depending on your model).

Childcare requirements, if childcare is part of your strategy— toys, games, floor mats, safety gates, cleaning supplies, along with professional background checks for volunteers.

Meal preparation supplies, if meals are part of your strategy—cooking and serving equipment, for example.

Storage containers where there is no permanent space—storage bins, rolling storage, etc.

In your planning with the team, write down the necessities, as well a "nice to have" list. You don't have to have all the one-time expenses sorted at the beginning, as it can happen in stages as the gathering grows and develops over time. Organize for the immediate needs based on the stage of your mission but keep orienting and organizing for where you want to be in the near future.

One-Time and Ongoing Expenses

Along with the initial start-up expenses, do your best to forecast the ongoing operational expenses. How much is needed to execute your fresh expression? To make it simple for planning purposes, a monthly budget and annual budget with categories will help give an accurate picture of the financial narrative.

Common Ongoing Expenses

Meals, snacks, and coffee

Dinnerware, utensils, and cleaning supplies

Childcare stipends and supplies

Teaching and discipleship materials (devotionals, Life Recovery Bibles, or any workbooks)

Office and administrative supplies

Rent for meeting space

I've encountered some amazing Fresh Expressions, including several I've coached, that faced the same question: how do we gain financial support to sustain the work? As the saying goes, "the God who gives the vision will also give the provision." The hard part for many of us is not asking God but asking people. So how can we prepare for this ministry of fundraising?

Communicating Vision with Clarity

Resources follow vision. People are motivated to give when they see a cause that is making a difference. Casting vision is not about telling people you need to pay the electric bill. That matters, but it's not compelling. What inspires generosity is clearly articulating the why behind your Fresh Expression. The "what" is your activities—what happens when you gather. The "why" is the heartbeat—

the prayers, the tears, and the motivation that keeps you going. It is important for the whole team to know the "why."

Keep your vision concise, not a dissertation.

Be ready with short transformation stories you can share "from your back pocket."

Sometimes you only get five minutes with a potential donor—make them count and be ready for the moment.

Multi-lane Funding Strategy

Don't limit funding to one source.

Develop Multiple Streams

- **Inherited churches or networks.** Missions committees, Sunday School classes, or small groups can provide financial support or in-kind donations.

  - What connections does your team have into these types of networks?

  - How can they share the vision and communicate the needs among their networks?

- **Denominational or network partners**: Some already have funds designated for new works.

- **Individual donors**: Friends of team members or those who are animated by a compassion for those navigating recover often give one-time or ongoing support because of relationships or shared passion.

- **Letter campaigns**: Old-school, but effective, especially when paired with follow-up conversations.

Remember that these efforts all flow out of relationship, not a hard sell. The saying goes: "If you ask for money, you get advice. If you ask for advice, you get money." Active listening is as important as casting vision.

Create In-Kind Partnerships

Businesses and nonprofits often want to invest in recovery. Ask around your greater networks to see if any businesses, organizations, and community foundations have contributed to either faith-based groups or recovery-oriented initiatives. They may not write a check, but they might provide meals, AV equipment, or supplies. At Fighting Chance Recovery, we partnered with a nonprofit of aspiring chefs who now cover 75 percent of our meals through in-kind donations. Another recovery expression partnered with the local food bank to prepare their meals.

Seek Grants and Creative Approaches

Grant-writing is another path. Someone on your team may have this skill—or know someone who does. Many grants exist at the local, state, or national level focused on recovery. In Ohio, for example, the governor's office funds faith-based recovery initiatives. As the opioid epidemic has skyrocketed, significant financial resources have been invested at the state-level that can flow down to nonprofits and faith communities. Most grantors require an annual budget, which underscores the importance of planning and budgeting.

Another creative approach is to treat your Fresh Expression like a new "birth." Spread the word, create an Amazon registry for one-time start-up expenses, and invite your network to help "stock the nursery."

There are numerous possibilities for fundraising events and initiatives. Don't just stick to one focus but diversify your approach.

Multiple strategies spread awareness, broaden support, and keep you steady if one avenue dries up.

Practicing Gratitude

The start-up phase to any work is exciting but can be a heavy lift in the beginning. Sustainability requires ongoing vision casting and relationship-building. Keep donors connected through updates, stories, and transformation highlights. Thank them promptly and personally. It has become my personal practice to send a letter to any first-time donor, write letters to all donors a few times a year, and make phone calls. Nothing can replace the personal touch, and nobody is going to be upset that you recognized their contributions.

Fundraising is ministry. And yes, administration is both ministry and a gift. Allow time for planning to take place but remember that perfection is not the goal...faithfulness is. With a team that shares diverse gifts—even budgeting, spreadsheets, and thank you notes—you can honor God, serve with compassion, and live out your vision for recovery community with intentionality and joy.

After each conversation, reflect on these questions:

What is the "why" behind our vision?

Can I hone it to articulate the "why" in one or two sentences?

Make a list of the people or organizations that come to mind that could potentially support this vision.

How can I cultivate gratitude and generosity, both in giving and receiving?

God of abundance, we know that you can do immeasurably more than we can ask for or imagine. We ask that you call and prepare people to walk beside us to care for the areas in our leadership that we need help in and those who are called to generously contribute to this work. We trust that you will provide not only the vision, but the resources to see the vision come to reality. Guide us in our conversations and allow us to know what to ask for and the timing of it. In Jesus' name, Amen.

Chapter 11

52-Week Commitment

And let us consider how we may spur one another on toward love and good deeds, not giving up meeting together, as some are in the habit of doing, but encouraging one another…

—Hebrews 10:24-25

It would have been easy to forego the Christmas Day service. Attendance would surely be low, and volunteers hard to come by. One leader and his spouse determined to show up and foster a space to share Christmas cookies, sing some Christmas carols, read the story of Jesus being born, and share about what it meant to them that the Son of God entered a messy world. As expected, attendance was exceedingly small. But among that handful of people was one young immigrant who had never attended before. He had come looking for community, needing to know that he was not alone on this day when he felt so far from family and so precarious in his current situation. But in a tiny conversation group eating sugar cookies together on Christmas, he began to be found by the love of God. That's the importance of a dedicated presence.

Why Consistent Presence Matters

Recovery isn't a linear path. It's full of good days, setbacks, deep questions, and fragile trust. The presence of a steady, grace-filled community is often what helps someone hold on—even when they're not sure what they believe. It says with your actions: "You matter enough for us to keep showing up."

Practical Ways to Build Consistent Presence

At the same time, consistent presence isn't easy. People are busy. Volunteers are sometimes hard to come by. Weeks fly by and it can feel hard to keep up. Therefore, it is important to think about sustainable community rhythms. If you create an expectation that every gathering is a big production, it is probably not going to be sustainable. So, let's consider a few guiding practices for teams who want to embody the ministry of regular, reliable presence in a recovery-centered community.

Plan for Year-Round Connection

Even when energy dips or attendance fluctuates, don't take a season off. Inconsistent rhythms not only create confusion, but they can also send the message that this community is shaped around convenience for the volunteers rather than the needs of those in recovery. How can you build a commitment to presence into your planning?

Build a year-round calendar with your team.

Plan in advance for holiday weeks, slow seasons, and vacation schedules.

Rotate leadership responsibilities to avoid burnout while maintaining consistency.

Offer Alternative Gatherings for Holidays & High-Stress Seasons

When traditional services might feel out of sync (e.g., Christmas, 4th of July), offer something relational, fun, and rooted in presence. For example:

Holiday Meals: Thanksgiving dinner, Christmas brunch, or a New Year's chili cook-off.

Game or Movie Nights: A relaxed space where laughter builds trust.

Cookouts & Park Gatherings: Recovery doesn't stop in summer—neither should your connection.

Grief & Gratitude Spaces: For holidays that are especially hard, create honest, reflective spaces.

Don't think of these as filler events. They're faithful expressions of belonging.

Be Flexible—but Show Up Anyway

If your musician cancels or your speaker can't make it, gather anyway. Sit in a circle. Read a Psalm. Pray for one another. Tell a story. Order pizza. The point is not performance—it's presence. Create a "low-lift" backup format for lean weeks (for example, story + prayer + communion). And train your team to pivot gracefully when plans fall through.

Build a Leadership Bench

Don't rely on one or two people. Train and empower a small team of leaders who can carry the vision together—so no one burns out and the presence stays strong. Presence is easier to sustain when it's a shared calling, not a solo act.

The God Who Doesn't Leave

In recovery ministry, we embody that promise—not just through teaching, but through time and life together. When we show up when it's hard, stay through the mess, and offer a consistent "yes" when people have learned to expect "no," we make God's promise tangible. To be sure, you won't always see the fruit right away. Some people will come once and disappear. Others will test your commitment, show up inconsistently, or walk away when it gets hard. But here's the thing: they're watching. And one day, when the bottom falls out or the fog lifts, they'll remember: "There's that church that's still showing up. I think I'll try again."

So, take heart. Even when it feels slow, your presence is a witness. Keep showing up. It matters more than you know.

What do you need to set in place now to strengthen your ability to have a regular presence?

God of Unfailing Presence,
Thank you for never giving up on us. Teach us to love with the
same steadiness—
not just when it's easy, but when it's messy and slow. Give us the
grace to keep showing up,
the courage to stay even when we lose confidence, and the joy of
seeing your quiet work unfolding in time. Make our presence a
reflection of yours. Faithful. Patient. Unconditional.
In Jesus' name we pray, Amen.

At the heart of the gospel is this promise: "Never will I
leave you. Never will I forsake you." – Hebrews 13:5

Becoming Community

Let us consider how we may spur one another on toward love and good deeds, not giving up meeting together... but encouraging one another.
— Hebrews 10:24–25

As we have communicated already, a Fresh Expression of Recovery is more than merely a one-hour worship service. It is impactful life-on-life transference. It is beloved community. A worship service is impactful, but it is not the only thing folks in recovery need on their spiritual journey. To be honest, it is not so much what we do when we are gathered as it who we are becoming together. Disciples are not just made in rows but in circles.

Walking Together

Discipleship in recovery happens both in groups and one-on-one. Sponsors are a much-encouraged lifeline among 12-step groups and are natural relational connections among any recovery mission. Yet you may want to also consider other mentoring relationships. For example, at Fighting Chance Recovery we invite people to seek a spiritual mentor in addition to their sponsor.

What's the difference?

Sponsor vs. Spiritual Mentor

Sponsor

Helps someone work the 12 Steps

Takes the 2 a.m. call

Doesn't have to be a Christian

Must advocate for the steps, speak truth, and encourage a spiritual path.

Spiritual Mentor

May not be an expert in recovery

Nurtures faith and biblical principles in everyday life

Practices may include reading Scripture, studying a book, praying, and celebrating milestones.

Over the years, I (Roz) have been blessed to mentor dozens of men, and every time I've received more than I gave. At Mosaic Church, the language of "spiritual mentor" has become part of our culture. We teach that it's the mentee's responsibility to initiate the relationship: making the initial ask, setting meetings, and deciding frequency. We've seen firsthand the power of these mentoring relationships for spurring spiritual growth. As a result, spiritual mentors are now so common at Mosaic Church that we host annual training for anyone interested.

A word of caution: if you engage in mentorship, your heart will be broken. Relapse is real, and it hurts everyone involved. But the seeds planted in mentoring are never wasted.

I've walked with men who relapsed, disappeared, and later returned to sobriety. One friend reconnected after a year away, finished his program, and has remained clean for years. If I had stayed stuck in my emotions, I might have missed what God was doing. Not every story ends that way, but when it does, it's a gift.

Mentorship isn't a one-way street. Mentors need the ministry as much, if not more, as the mentees. Walking with others reminds us of our own dependence on grace. I grow in my own walk with Jesus as I encourage others in their faith journey. Spiritual mentoring is reciprocal—healing flows both ways, and both grow deeper in Christ.

One more reality to acknowledge: recovery communities are often transient. People may be here today and gone tomorrow. But again, it's not about us—it's about faithfully scattering seeds and trusting God with the harvest.

Outside Partnerships

While we encourage to people to be part of the faith community, we also understand it can be a bridge to other healing communities such as Alcoholics Anonymous (AA), Narcotics Anonymous (NA), etc. Everyone's journey is different. Some do not participate in meetings and others swear by them. Research has shown that those who actively engage in these kinds of healing communities have a better chance with longevity in their recovery.

Practical Steps for Partnership

Provide a list of group meetings (with dates, times, and locations) to provide for those seeking these needed connections.

Compile a living document as you hear about various meetings and groups.

Print copies and have digital versions ready for you and the team to share.

If the leadership comes together, it is not uncommon for such a group to branch off your own Fresh Expression recovery community. Mosaic Church, for example, hosts one of the longest standing NA groups in all of Ohio every Friday night. If launching your own group isn't possible, open your facility to outside groups. You don't have to reinvent the wheel—partner with what God is already doing in your community.

Having Fun as a Community

Discipleship is more than Bible study—it's life together. That means showing people in recovery that faith communities can laugh, play, and celebrate.

Examples from Fighting Chance Recovery

Game Nights: Game nights inject some play and connection within our community. On these nights, chairs are cleared, board games come out, and laughter fills the room. Some sip coffee and watch, others jump into larger group games, cornhole tournaments, karaoke, or "Recovery Jeopardy." Game nights help us to break stereotypes: sobriety is not boring, and neither is church.

Outdoor Events: We also host cookouts, outdoor worship, and bonfires where testimonies flow freely over s'mores. These moments create joy and belonging alongside spiritual growth.

Seasons and Sacred Moments

Liturgical seasons provide opportunities to deepen faith and connect with those who may find more natural times to step into the community and explore.

Lent

Lent is a season that resonates strongly with the recovery journey. The season inherently invites people to surrender and pursue God wholeheartedly, a posture that has deep meaning for those in the process of surrendering their addiction. Ash Wednesday sets the course for this season, as we experience the significance of ashes, and encounter a God who wants to turn our brokenness into something beautiful.

Christmas

Christmas is a ripe season for deepening a sense of joy and connection. We recognize that it can be a difficult season for those in recovery, due to increased stress, exposure to triggers like alcohol, feelings of loneliness and isolation, and potential family conflicts. Therefore, we know how important it is to provide a safe and hopeful community in which the joy of the season can be experienced. We have also found that this season provides natural opportunities to extend special invitations to the wider community.

Experiment often and do not be afraid to teach people about the Christian faith and story to help strengthen their sobriety.

Becoming, Not Just Attending

A Fresh Expression of Recovery is not just a service—it's a community of people becoming more like Jesus. It's also more than a support group—it's an invitation into new life. The invitation is not merely to attend but to become. At Fighting Chance, we've witnessed faith commitments and baptisms. We've seen whole families reconciled and restored. We've seen leaders rise up to lead ministries and nonprofits, and servants rise up to join mission trips. And we get a front row seat to disciples of Jesus who are on fire, more animated in their life with Christ as it overflows in service to others than ever before in their lives. This is the heart of recovery discipleship: transformation, not just participation.

After each conversation, reflect on these questions:

How can I shift from having a mentality of hosting a service to practicing being a community and disciples of Jesus Christ?

Who might I invite into a spiritual mentoring relationship, with me as mentor or mentee?

What is one way I can help foster joy, fun, and connection in our recovery community this month?

Almighty God, you have called us to walk together in community and not just live this life on our own. May we seek to be more than just a gathering of people but a community that embodies your Spirit that we can grow together in love and laughter. Allow us to be unified as a people with one body, one spirit, and one baptism to serve the world and community you have called us to love. In Jesus' name, Amen.

Chapter 13

Multiply the Mission

So deeply do we care for you that we are determined to share with you not only the gospel of God but also our own selves, because you have become very dear to us.

—*1 Thessalonians 2:8 (NRSVUE)*

To be honest, "Joe" started coming just for the free meal. Then he stayed for the stories and the sense that "these people get me." Eventually, he started to talk about the community as family. Then he asked for prayer. Then he brought a friend. Then he showed up early to help set up chairs. Then he asked to be baptized and shared his story of faith coming alive. One day, he approached the team and asked, "How can I help others?"

This is the slow and beautiful rhythm of multiplication in a recovery church community. What begins as healing for one person becomes a source of hope for many. And when we make space for that transformation to take root, not just in personal recovery but in someone's emerging life with Jesus, we begin to see something extraordinary: disciples who make disciples and communities that give birth to new communities.

The Outflow of the Gospel

Healing is not just for us—it's meant to flow through us.

For those who are working the 12 Steps, it should come as no surprise that profound spiritual awakening leads to a life of pouring into others. This is, after all, the heart of Step 12.

In the twelfth step, you are urged to pause and contemplate the spiritual awakening that has been cultivated throughout your journey across these twelve steps. Recovery for all of us is submitting our will to the care of God.

As we invite God to take control of our lives and will, God will give us peace in difficult situations, heightened compassion toward others when we are in disagreements, and the ability to empathize with others who are going through challenges.[1]

When someone who has been set free by Christ begins to use their life to bless others, the kingdom expands in visible ways. This is what we long for: a front row seat to hope and new creation rippling out.

Building a Culture of Multiplication

But here's the truth: multiplication doesn't happen by accident. It happens when we cultivate a culture of participation, empowerment, and ownership. And that means we must name it, nurture it, and normalize it.

When John Nevius was called into missions in Korea, he was convinced that the emerging gospel community was more likely to thrive if those who were becoming disciples of Jesus were empowered to take ownership of the emerging community. This posture, radical at the time, was meant to discourage dependance on the foreign missionary, and empower the indigenous community to shape the mission. Nevius encouraged the "three-self principle": that the mission should quickly become self-governing, self-supporting, and self-propagating. In other words, Nevius knew that if the gospel was

---

1. Step 12 as adapted and outlined in *A Fighting Chance in 40 Days: 12 Steps to a New Life in Jesus* by Rosario Picardo (Invite Press, 2024), pg. 160.

to grow in that setting, it would need to ripple out from the gospel witness and commitment of its local members. History reveals that Nevius was perhaps one of the most fruitful missionaries of his time. Perhaps that's because he named, nurtured, and normalized a culture in which people coming to faith would be the best ambassadors of Christ in their everyday lives.

We don't want to accidentally create a culture of religious consumers. Instead, we want to see people coming into a vibrant, substance free life with Jesus, following his voice into the everyday spaces and relationships in their life. Jesus challenged his disciples: "As the Father sent me, so I am sending you." (John 20:21 CEB) We must do likewise or instead of disciples who create disciples, we will see an emergence of program attenders who merely consume what is offered for them. So how do we go about setting this kind of culture?

Start with Discipleship, Not Just Attendance

If we treat people as attenders, they'll attend.

If we treat people as observers, they'll observe.

If we treat people as disciples-in-progress, they'll grow.

How are we inviting people to grow in faith, not just attend events? Do we have simple ways to invite folks into Scripture, prayer, and service? Are we creating low-pressure, high-love environments where people can take next steps spiritually?

Name the Calling You See in Others and Offer Ways to Serve

Find out people's skills, passions, and hobbies, and enlist them to serve. Whether it is assembling hygiene kits, cleaning a park, or doing home repairs, there is no such thing as an insignificant service.

Many people don't see themselves as leaders or valuable contributors. Especially those in recovery who carry shame, trauma, or self-doubt. That's why we need to be prophetic encouragers, naming the good we see: "You have a gift for making people feel welcome." "I think others would benefit from your story." "Would you pray about helping lead something?"

Multiplication often begins with a trusted voice coming alongside and communicating: "I see something in you."

Make Space for New Expressions to Emerge

Sometimes, the Spirit births a whole new expression of church among a particular group—led by someone whose faith was shaped within your community. In a previous chapter you heard about one participant of Fighting Chance who started a Thursday Night Live faith community in a treatment and vocational center. But there are other examples, as well:

- A young man in recovery starts a weekly basketball-and-Bible night with other men in sober living.

- A woman who is parenting her grandchildren gathers other caregivers for prayer and encouragement.

- A small group forms around hiking, storytelling, and Scripture, led by someone whose faith came alive outdoors.

It's often surprising what the Holy Spirit is stirring, so pay attention when individuals begin to share ideas and connections. Take the opportunity to bless the impulse, explore together what God might be up to, and help people experiment in love.

Support Their First Steps

Emerging leaders often need:

- Encouragement and spiritual support: regular check ins and prayer time can be invaluable to a new and emerging leader.

- A simple leadership "buddy" or mentor: effective leadership skills can be nurtured and developed through companionship and mentoring.

- A place to try and fail without shame: there is no mission experimentation without risks, so reframe "failure" as simply a chance to learn something that can be applied to the next experiment. This provides a healthy environment to take risks for the sake of the gospel.

- A clear "yes" from the larger community: knowing that the wider community celebrates your efforts and is cheering you on can put wind in the sails of an emerging leader.

You may want to keep a list of "starter experiments" that people could try, whether that be meals, acts of service, or new gatherings. Make it a point to spend some time with an emerging leader, helping them discern what might be a good fit for their gifts and passion. And along the way, provide a sounding board to hone ideas, a supportive community of prayer, and talking partners to process the celebrations and disappointments.

The Trajectory of Multiplication

Picture this scenario: James begins showing up weekly to your recovery church community. He is quiet, steady, and quick to help stack chairs at the end. One day, a team member pulls him aside and says, "You have a pastor's heart. Would you help check in on a few others during the week?" Notice that here a trusted voice has called out something he sees in James, which gives James the ability to see ways he could meaningfully contribute to the community. James starts calling three people. Then he calls five more. Seeing his gifts in connecting with others and encouraging them in the faith, a team member inquires if James might be open to co-leading a small group. In this co-leadership role, James is mentored by a leader who has some experience leading a small group, while at the same time exercising his own natural gifts. A year later, James is helping host a Sunday night gathering in a halfway house because he is now animated in his deeper purpose to pour into others, he has incrementally been invited into deeper service, and he has been supported and mentored to develop his leadership.

As people encounter Jesus, they are empowered to embody Christ's love in new places, among new people. When we expect this, nurture this, and create space for it, we begin to see the kingdom multiplied—one life, one gathering, one ripple at a time.

Ask:

Who are we discipling?

Who are we encouraging?

What new forms of church might God be planting through the people we're walking with now?

God of the Mustard Seed,
You take our small beginnings and grow something so much more.
So we ask you to raise up leaders from unlikely places. Give us eyes
to see the gifts in others, and courage to call them forth. Teach us to
trust the little seeds that you might grow into new communities of
grace. Multiply your mission through us, Lord. Not for our name,
but for yours. In Jesus' name, Amen.

Every healing life contains seeds of new community. Let's
be quick to notice and nourish those seeds by gently calling forth the potential in others.

Chapter 14

Sent With Courage: A Commission for Recovery Ministry

We are therefore Christ's ambassadors, as though God were making his appeal through us.

—2 Corinthians 5:20

It is a holy and sacred calling to start and lead a recovery faith community. While it may be some of the most difficult work you will ever engage in, it also has the potential to be some of the most transformative.

Over and over again, we have seen the soil of people's lives most open to the gospel when they come to the end of themselves, recognizing that they can control neither their lives nor their future. They recognize that they need a Savior and Jesus meets them in their desperation. This makes the recovery journey a significant opportunity for the gospel to take root. Yet addiction is a seductive temptress, so any faith community working with those in recovery or families impacted by addiction will also navigate some heartbreak along the way. We encourage you to step into this work with both eyes wide open and hearts wide open. If God is calling you into this mission, then God will be with you in this mission.

Being in deep community with those who have experienced the pain of addiction will change you. You will likely discover what it means to be raw and real before God and with each other, perhaps more than any other "churchy" setting you've been a part of. There is no pretending and no cliches as, together, you learn to trust Jesus to give you strength for the next hour, the next day, and the next week. You will discover there is beautiful power in confessing brokenness and finding God's embrace right there. Don't be surprised that this kind of faith community will impact your life as much as the lives you hoped to impact.

We have tried to give you some practical handholds as you consider how God may be sending you or your congregation into mission. It's likely that we frustrated you in the early chapters, as most people just want the checklist to effective Recovery Church, and instead we invited you into a process of listening, praying, and connecting relationships. Yet, in our experience, "unless the LORD builds the house, the builders labor in vain." (Psalm 127:1) It may seem counterintuitive to start by slowing down, but it is this process that allows us to walk in step with God. God knows better than we do what kind of community is needed, so it is folly for us to try to do this with merely human strategy and effort.

We also cannot advocate more emphatically how critical it is to enter this kind of mission with others. You will burn out if you try to do this alone. Build a team shaped by love and grace. Share the load of these efforts; you can accomplish far more as a group than as one passionate prophet trying to take on the world! Not only that, the quality of relationships among a team is the seed for the emerging community. The way that you love, pray, and dream together will give life to a community that loves, prays, and dreams together. The way you forgive one another and call forth the best of one another will set the tone for a community that faithfully navigates the inevitable messiness of human relationships in the Way of Jesus.

We also want to remind you: it is progress over perfection. There is no perfect model out there. What matters the most is the consistency to show up in relationships, faithfulness, and presence. So don't wait until you have every detail figured out or think that everything must be perfect on paper to get started. You just need to know enough to take the next intentional step, knowing that from time to time you will hit a challenge or setback that will require you to shift your next steps. Notice, pray, consider alternatives, get some input or feedback, and then take another step.

Finally, trust that the Lord is already at work in the everyday spaces where the strongholds of addiction are being dismantled. Jesus himself, echoing the words of the prophet Isaiah, proclaimed that we could recognize signs of God's kingdom where we see captives being freed and the brokenhearted being healed. (Luke 4:18-19, Isaiah 61:1) When we join up with these efforts, we can know that we are partnering with God's intention for the renewal of all things.

A Prayer of Commissioning

Lord Jesus,
You came to heal the brokenhearted and set captives free.
We offer ourselves to your mission among those in recovery.
Give us your heart—gentle and fierce, truthful and kind.
Grant us wisdom to listen well, courage to love without fear,
and perseverance when the road is long.
Protect our team with unity, joy, and holy rest.
Raise up leaders from within the recovery community.
Let hope take root and lives be made new.
Build what only you can build, for your glory, and use us as co-
laborers for the sake of your kingdom.
In the name of the Father, Son, and Holy Spirit. Amen.

Go with a Christ-like tenderness and a courageous love—
patient, truthful, and resilient.
See the image of God in every person.
Learn names and stories.
Celebrate small victories.
Measure success by faithfulness, not acclaim.
The Spirit who called you will supply wisdom, compassion,
and strength for the journey.

Appendix

Sample Session Flow Guide

Every Fresh Expression will have its own unique "flavor" and "challenges." As discussed throughout this book, every decision should be based on listening conversations. Below is a sample session flow to guide your team through the process. Each step is framed and shaped by what questions we would begin with if we were in the room with your team, coaching you through the process. These questions are collected from each chapter and are not the only questions that you might ask, but they are designed to inspire conversations and get your team talking about what they see, what they hear, and where God is leading throughout the process. Please note that this is not a single session, nor are any of the steps representative of a single session. Listening takes time, and so does reflection and discernment.

Purpose

Planting Hope Here seeks to equip ministry teams, lay people, clergy, and church planters to plant Jesus-centered communities of recovery. Each section weaves in theology, missiological principles, story, and practice in the different stages of development starting with listening all the way to launching.

1. Begin with a Listening Posture

Cultivate prayerful practices to discern where God is already at work along with a posture of humility, listening, learning, and presence.

- Where has God raised your awareness or compassion during a prayer walk?

- What places or locations have drawn you and the team to cover in prayer?

- Where did you sense God's presence?

2. Listening Deeply in the Community

Enter into conversations with those engaged in the work of recovery, have been impacted by addiction, or are in recovery themselves.

- What surprised me in what I heard?

- Where did my assumptions get challenged?

- What are my big takeaways?

- What is God saying to me?

3. Assess the Needs and Opportunities

Discern what already exists, identify gaps, where to partner, and asset mapping of can be possible.

- What strengths and assets already exist in your community?

- What breaks your heart or won't leave you alone?

- Where do you sense the Spirit's gentle invitation?

4. Building the Team

Prayerfully form a diverse, Spirit-led team that reflects your mission field.

- Who needs to be invited to be part of the team?
- What should be a regular part of your meetings to foster an aligned, healthy team?
- How will you deepen the bonds of your team?

5. Crafting the Table

Shape the gathering with both experimentation and collaboration with those in recovery where context is the main driver and not preference.

- In what ways am I inviting others into leadership rather than creating something on my own?
- What values do we sense are important for this emerging community?
- What elements that were described in this chapter resonate with your team and which ones don't? What other elements might be important in your context?

6. Pick Your Path

Choose a model that fits your context.

- After considering the discernment questions around the models, what direction is a good fit for your context and why?
- What non-negotiable theological or spiritual values have emerged as you think about your community?
- What voices from the recovery community are we incorporating at this stage? What are we hearing and how does that hone the direction we need to take?

7. Good News in the Midst of Recovery

Share the gospel in contextually relevant ways for those who are on a journey of healing.

- Where do I see some of the spiritual themes in this chapter in my own life, and how might that shape the way I walk alongside those in recovery?

- What aspects of the good news of Jesus would I add to this list that might particularly resonate with those navigating recovery?

- How comfortable am I with my own weakness and vulnerability? In what ways could modeling that be a gift to those navigating recovery?

8. Consider Additional Elements

Determine what holistic support looks like around the worshipping community.

- What additional element might your team need to consider at this stage of the mission and why?

- What would be needed to bring that element to life?

- How could you start bringing those dreams and needs before the Lord?

9. Where Vision Meets Reality

Translate the vision into practical steps.

- What practical needs (space, schedule, meal, childcare) do I need to plan for in our FX Recovery?

- How might I shift from an "us and them" mindset to true community co-creation?

- Is there any detail that you and your team can investigate to help people feel seen, welcomed, heard, and valued?

10. Fueling The Vision

Sustain the mission through prayer, partnerships, and provision.

- What is the "why" behind our vision? Can I hone it to articulate the "why" in one or two sentences?
- Make a list of the people or organizations that come to mind that could potentially support this vision?
- How can I cultivate gratitude and generosity, both in giving and receiving?

52-Week Commitment

Recovery Ministry is about consistency and commitment.

- What do you need to set in place now to strengthen your ability to have a regular presence?

Becoming Community

Move from simply hosting an event to becoming a family.

- How can I shift from having a mentality of hosting a service to practicing being a community and disciples of Jesus Christ?

- Who might I invite into a spiritual mentoring relationship, with me as mentor or mentee?

- What is one way I can help foster joy, fun, and connection in our recovery community this month?

Multiply the Mission

What God begins in one community can ripple outward to form another one.

- Who are we discipling?
- Who are we encouraging?
- What new forms of church might God be planting through the people we're walking with now?

The 12 Steps:
Fighting Chance Edition[1]

1. Admit powerlessness

2. Embrace trust

3. Find strength in surrender

4. Embrace self-reflection

5. Admit our wrongdoings

6. Confront our flaws

7. Pursue wisdom

8. Seek peace

9. Make amends

10. Embrace daily reflection

11. Seek God's will daily

12. Share changes

---

1. This list of the 12 Steps is as adapted and outlined in *A Fighting Chance in 40 Days: 12 Steps to a New Life in Jesus* by Rosario Picardo (Invite Press, 2024).

www.ingramcontent.com/pod-product-compliance
Lightning Source LLC
Chambersburg PA
CBHW020409130626
46549CB00006B/2495